WHEN
— THE —
LIGHTS
— ARE —
BRIGHT
AGAIN

WHEN THE — LIGHTS — ARE BRIGHT AGAIN

Letters and images of loss, hope, and resilience from the theater community

CREATED BY **ANDREW NORLEN**
PHOTOGRAPHY BY **MATTHEW MURPHY**

APPLAUSE
THEATRE & CINEMA BOOKS
GUILFORD, CONNECTICUT

APPLAUSE
THEATRE & CINEMA BOOKS

An imprint of Globe Pequot, the trade division of The Rowman & Littlefield Publishing Group, Inc.
4501 Forbes Blvd., Ste. 200
Lanham, MD 20706
ApplauseBooks.com

Distributed by NATIONAL BOOK NETWORK

Cover and book design by Asya Blue Design

Photo Retouching: Evan Zimmerman

whenthelightsarebrightagain.com

British Library Cataloguing in Publication Information available

Library of Congress Cataloging-in-Publication Data available

ISBN 978-1-4930-6659-9 (hardcover)
ISBN 978-1-4930-6660-5 (e-book)

♾™ The paper used in this publication meets the minimum requirements of American National Standard for Information Sciences–Permanence of Paper for Printed Library Materials, ANSI/NISO Z39.48-1992

for the ones we lost,

for the hope we fight for,

for the resilience in each of us.

---

for Nick Cordero.

Contents

FOREWORD

by Andrew Norlen

Light (noun): the natural agent that stimulates sight and makes things visible.

It is October, 2020. I am 2,881 miles away from my city, my job, my home, my career, my chosen family, and above all else—my dream.

We are now eight months into a global pandemic, ravaged by a virus that has no political or economic bias—no—this virus will affect you whether you believe in it or not.

I am back in my roots, deep inside my roots. Living within the four walls that held a deep and painful secret for all of my adolescence, until I left the nest and headed East. There, I was able to grow up and discover the me I wished to be inside this collective we've named "life."

This house holds my secrets, or it used to, I should say. But now, eight months into this new normal called Covid-19, I think I am starting to unlearn parts of my strength that I've grown up, and into, during my twenties back East. I don't like this. I don't like feeling this regression. I don't like feeling out of control, not that I ever had any before the virus, but the illusion was comforting. Maybe.

As I sit down to dinner tonight with my parents, I've started to finally see them as fully human. No more heroic pedestal: they are simply imperfect, fallible, broken, beautiful, and complicated adults—just like me. It's as if I've watched the perfect parents of my mind vanish to reveal two people, who are so much more like me than I ever realized as a child.

As we begin to eat the meal my mom has prepared, I feel my anxiety welling up within me. It sits at the top of my throat, shaking, angry, fearful, and overwhelmed. "What's wrong bud?" My dad asks, as they both sit with my aggressive and pulsating energy. And then my rant releases itself unto our table:

"I just hate this! All of it! I don't know what to do with myself! I miss dancing, but I don't want to take a class online cause it hurts too much, and it's not the same. I feel so much guilt for not reaching out to my friends and engaging to see what they are up to, something keeps stopping me. I am so tired of listening to everyone and their mother say, 'What's your plan Andrew?' 'What are you going to do when you can get back to the city?' I can't stand how the world just sees artists as disposable, telling us to pivot and change professions and career paths, like that choice is as easy as picking out an ice cream flavor or something? It's infuriating. I'm drowning in student loans that I'm going to be paying off till the day I die, and the world thinks that my profession is laughable and so easily remedied. When does all of the hard work get to feel worth it? I wish I had a person to share this difficult time with. At this point I'm convinced that I will always be alone. And even as I say that out loud, I feel so selfish and ridiculous and guilty, because people are dying in the world, and who am I to complain?! I have a roof over my head, and food on the table. I don't know. I guess I just feel like I have no purpose. And I hate that so much of who I am is wrapped up in what I do."

The next morning I FaceTime my best friend Kenna. As I begin to tell her about my embarrassing rant with my parents over dinner last night, which essentially is now just a rerun episode of that same rant, but louder, with a mask on, and on a stair-climber at the gym down the street. She interrupts me…

"Bubba, why don't you write it down? You write everything else down!" She says,

I pause. Filled with chills head to toe.

"Like, what if you wrote a letter to yourself? Or like, a letter to the industry? About what you miss. Like when we write an email that we never send, but it just feels good to speak it out. You know?"

Again, full chills. These weren't nerves, they weren't fear, and they weren't apprehension. As she speaks I have a moment of alignment inside me, but I don't yet know what it means.

"Shit. I love that!" I blurt out. "I gotta go! I'll call you tomorrow."

I hang up and my wheels start spinning. The ideas won't stop flowing. My mind races for a solid 48 hours and I don't sleep a wink. I have 10+ ideas for a title, but one keeps sticking out…..*When The Lights Are Bright Again*. Every time I say it out loud, or read it, I get that feeling again, the same chills from before. The more I think about this idea of writing down how I feel, the more I keep thinking to myself…

"I need to do this. Wait—we all need to do this."

————————

And just like that, this book became a reality before it was ever anything physical. In one moment I made a choice inside and I remember thinking: "If I do this right, this could change the world." That thought still gives me the same effervescent goosebumps today—even as I write this—that it gave me the day I created the book inside my dreams. I had no idea what this book would look like, but in the fraction of an instant I found purpose. My purpose was to give everyone who wanted

a space to rant, rage, grieve, lament, praise, rejoice or exclaim that same space, that platform, the same way that my best friend Kenna had just given me permission to release. I wasn't willing to stop until I created that space for everyone.

The ironic thing was I became so invested in the creation of this book that I continued to put off writing my own letter. I worked on the book for almost six months before I ever wrote a word or thought about writing my own letter at all. Sure, I had found a purpose inside of this idea, but I instead chose to silence and pivot my focus onto the task of creating, instead of the actual act of creating from *within* myself. For myself.

The Actors Fund was fresh in my mind after a friend shared with me that they had helped him pay his bills for two or three months during the summer of 2020. This amazed me, and I did some digging and got in contact with Douglas Ramirez at TAF. I will never forget our first phone call, when I pitched the book idea to him and he said, "Andrew I'm so sorry to interrupt you, but I have chills and I'm wiping tears from my eyes. I have heard a LOT of ideas for fundraisers all year, but nothing like this. This is special." The book was leading the charge—I was not.

Next, I knew I wanted this coffee table book to have images, but I had no idea how I would manage to accomplish that without asking someone for help. My sister kept teasing me because I kept saying I wanted it to be a coffee table book, but had no plans of who would take the photos. Matthew Murphy immediately came to mind the more I thought about it, as he took my cast's production photos for the closing company of the Kinky Boots national tour. I reached out to Matthew, and he quickly agreed to be a part of the project before ever really having a full understanding of what was before us. He loved the idea, and jumped in with a "Yes!" The more I think about this now, the more I start to wonder if maybe the power of this project, outside of my own control, inspired Matthew to see purpose in himself and the possibilities for our community within this book, and maybe that led him to his "Yes!"

I owe him the world! Thank you won't ever be enough.

So after nearly a year at home under my parents' roof, my body was telling me it was time to return to NYC, in whatever stage the city was in and restart my life again. So that's what I did.

In March of 2021, I moved back to Manhattan and began manifesting the life I have always wanted here–yet often found myself much too afraid to truly step into. I spent months getting my house in order and decorated the way I wanted it. Home and peace and my environment have become paramount in my life. I kept chipping away at the book with Matthew and making our plans to self-publish whenever Broadway reopened.

One afternoon, I noticed a coffee table book that I have had for years resting in my living room. When I was a senior in high school my dear friend, mentor, 2nd mom, past theater director and former NYC dweller, Katherine, gifted me this book when I was headed East for school. (Also, check out her letter in CONNECTION!) In the front of the book she wrote a beautiful note where she encouraged me to never stop until I fulfilled my dreams. One afternoon, I flipped this book over and saw that it was published by Applause Books, and, you guessed it...my wheels started spinning.

I emailed their general info@ email, and kept going about my day's to-do list. Twenty minutes later, a man named John emailed me and said, "Andrew, I have just watched your pitch video for your book. This project is very intriguing to me. Can I call you right now?" I got the full body chills again and did the only thing I knew how to, emailed him back with a "Yes!"

He called, and we talked for an hour. I was late to work that day, but I didn't care one bit, because another person had heard about this book–someone that had the ability to take it to the next level, to help even more people. (Cue chills!) We talked and talked about how I came up with this, and also how behind we were in terms of timeline in the publishing world if we were ever going to entertain getting this thing picked up and sent out to the globe. But John still believed in it. He said a few times, "It will be really hard, but it's not impossible."

A month later, Applause graciously picked it up, and Matthew, myself, and our amazing team (that we built right after I hung up the phone that day with John) got to work. We spent five fast and furious weeks shooting, editing, reaching out, marketing and connecting with our community to create what you are holding right now.

If I hadn't trusted my gut telling me it was time to go back to NYC and start again, I would never have unpacked my boxes from storage...I would never have discovered the coffee table book from Katherine in my living room...or reached out to John to partner with Applause.

You are exactly where you are supposed to be. Always. Even when that is hard to trust or believe in at all, lean into it and simply pause, to truly see.

I started this foreword by sharing the definition of "light." I always find myself returning to the meaning of words, because I think words matter–enormously. What we call each other, how we speak to ourselves, our identity. Words have power. Words have influence. We sure as hell have learned this in a massive way during the last four years politically in the United States.

The experience of creating this book from an idea inside my head into the pages you are reading right now has been one of the hardest and, yet, most gratifying moments of my entire life. I can explain all of it in one word: Community.

This book never would've happened without me getting out of my own way, getting out of my own head, humbling myself, silencing my ego, and reaching out to other artists and asking them to come and join me to live inside of their sweet spot, and shine! To me, that is community; that is the theater; that is light!

This time has been so close to the definition of light: Stimulating sight and making things visible.

Let us turn this much-needed, long-overdue, grand reckoning into the new renaissance we all so deserve.

I'll leave you with the letter that might have taken me six months to get around to writing, but with the words that found me exactly when I needed them the most...

> "Relish in the moment you are having right now, reading your own words, in a letter, inside a book–a book filled to the spine with love, and passion, and loss, and grief, and anger, and hope. **Always hope.**"

ANDREW NORLEN
Originally from
Troutdale, OR

Dear Andrew,

When the lights are bright again, the fear you feel right now will also be a mere fragment in history.

Your journey to writing this letter to yourself–for yourself–is the perfectly broken picture of the grief you've been darting and dodging away from.

When the virus came, you were forced to face the viruses in your own backyard, your own tribe, your own industry, your own family. It was a confrontation that you could not fix, mend, or bandage with your usual hustle, smile, or big ideas–there wasn't an answer this time. It was time for you to listen. To learn. To unlearn. To elevate. To educate. To speak up.

When days turned into weeks, your mind began to wander and warn your soul to prepare for a bumpy ride.

When weeks turned into months, you found solace in helping others make their house a home–but inside you wondered when you might have a home again yourself.

When months turned into seasons, you packed your life away into a box, locked the door, and turned your back toward a paused dream you feared might never be revived.

When seasons became a year, your body realized it had learned everything it could inside of memories and past and family–it was time to be alone again. To be uncomfortable again. To change again. To grow again. To be brave–again.

I learned these affirmations:

- I am not my job, but my job IS a job.

- I am whole just by waking up in the morning.

- I am worthy of greatness, but greatness defined by me.

- I am responsible to wield my privilege for good, for kindness, for humanity.

- I am beyond lucky to bring others joy for a living. That is a gift.

- I am enough, no matter who I am with, what I do, or how much $ is in my name.

- I am on this earth to make others feel seen and proud of themselves–but I can't do that until I feel the same way about the man in my own mirror.

When The Lights Are Bright Again…

When: When is the hope. The knowing inside all of us that our industry is way too strong to be extinguished forever.

The Lights: The lights are the people. An industry built on the immediacy of a moment. A shared experience that is transient, effervescent, cathartic and once in a lifetime. Magic.

Bright: Bright is everyone we've lost. We have been dimmed in reality and we have been dimmed in spirit. We honor those who never again get to share their bright light with our community. The magic is that their impact is immortal.

And, Again: Again represents that the lights were once bright before this time, but when we do return, we must return differently. We must learn from every uncomfortable conversation we've had. We must fight for equity, fight for the hard conversations, fight for the representation, fight for the equal pay, and fight for the marginalized.

What we were doing before wasn't working, before the virus came. But, the lesson it leaves behind is that when you don't confront the virus in your own heart, your own job, your own family, your own industry–the virus will confront you. I promise.

When the lights are bright again, just pause. Relish in the moment you are having right now, reading your own words, in a letter, inside a book–a book filled to the spine with love, and passion, and loss, and grief, and anger, and hope. Always hope.

You did this–no–WE did this!
The lights could never be bright again without the WE.

Be proud of this moment Andrew. Give yourself the permission slip to indulge for five or ten minutes–and then get back to the work.

The work is where we create to find the answers we won't ever fully comprehend.

We can do hard things.
Be well. Be kind. And be brave.
1-4-3
__Andrew__

TIME

Dear Megan,

When the lights are bright again, your dreams will only shine brighter.

This past (almost) year has been difficult–filled with loss, uncertainty, frustration and some of the lowest lows you've ever seen. However, this pause has also given you the precious gift of time. Time to slow down, time to reflect, extra time to spend with family, time to revisit and hone in on old or underdeveloped skills and time to learn new ones. Time to revisit relationships, strengthen bonds and grow an even stronger admiration to your community/chosen family that have helped you through these lows.

When the lights are bright again you will be grateful; grateful for the break to breathe and rest and grow and learn. When the lights are bright again you will take this newfound growth, strength and inspiration and run with it - living your life to the fullest, loving with your whole heart and always being present in every moment.

When the lights are bright again you will come back stronger, remembering your why and using it to motivate you. Because even though it's been (almost) a year, you still remember that feeling you get when you see others happy, engaged and experiencing shared joy, together.

When the lights are bright again you will be ready; ready to shine. I know because I know your secret– you stay ready; **you've always been ready**.

Grateful and hopeful,
Megan
@_meganl
Originally from Alameda, CA

Dear Ghost Light,

When the lights are bright again, caring won't be over.

Our love for one another and others will continue.

We have learned that there aren't just peaks and valleys in life, but waves.

A sea of emotions and experiences we paddle out to catch.

Then one current takes us away.

We get led astray then back to join our friends.

"What did I miss?"

Did I miss alot? Or did I just miss everyone sitting in the water, making sure we all made it.

We will make it, Ghost Light.

When the lights are bright again, we will be at the theatre and look forward, backwards, behind us, under us and say, "Everyone is here."

And we will ride the waves. Swim stronger against currents that disrupt us.

Because in the end we all will be together, ready to take a box for those who are watching from the shores.

We will love, Ghost Light.

Our hearts will be fuller. Our eyes will speak deeper. Our presence will sit fuller in spaces where we once occupied.

A full house of people will mean a fuller heart. And an empty theatre will mean full possibilities for us all.

We still have so many stories to tell, Ghost Light. So many voices to hear speak. And so many spaces to share with others.

When the lights are bright again, the Ghost Light will remain bright, lighting the way through the darkness. So many possibilities.

Holding onto hope,
Ghost Light
@jackson.Cooper.arts
Originally from Seattle, WA

Dear Patrick,

When the lights are bright again, never forget the strength that this time brought you. You are so much stronger than you can even imagine.

Remember the joy you found in looking up at the sun and moon. Seeing the stars again. Taking the time to truly be present and breathe into the moment.

Never forget that this time showed you the deep love for the stage. Don't question yourself. Be thankful for the many hours you were able to inspire other students and teach the art form that you love with a burning passion.

What was a time of struggle and pain for the world, brought so much strength and growth at the same time. Keep looking upward and to the future of what our industry can, and will be. The deep connection of artists is what drives so much of the beauty in the world around you.

Hold on to the countless phone conversations and memories with your friends, family, and community. The calls that brought tears, smiles, longing, anticipation for a new day. Even in the moments when you miss embracing those around you…. this valuable time may never come again.

Be thankful for every moment that you get to perform, whether on a computer at home or the many times coming when our stages are shining again. Your worth is not in the number of performances, but in the joy you create each morning and share with the world.

There is so much good around us.

Holding on for a brighter day for us all,
Patrick
@mrpatrickg
Originally from Lexington, KY

> " When the lights are bright again, we will be at the theatre and **look forward, backwards, behind us, under us** and say, **"Everyone is here."** "

Dear Amanda,

When the lights are bright again, you will get your creative light back. The light is still on but it is dim. Do acknowledge your feeling of creative loss and remember it during all those early student matinees and long tech days. Think of how many times you'll say "Omg remember 2020?" or "At least it's not 2020!" Also think of your brightest light, Addison, your almost two-year-old firecracker of a girl. The light is in her smile, her laugh and the wonder in her eyes. This has been a really hard year that you'll certainly never forget but your girl made it amazing. She showed you how strong she really can be at such a young age. It'll be great getting back to work but wasn't it the best summer?! All the new things you got to show her! All the new things she learned! When was the last time you had a summer off? **Take care of yourself so you can take care of others.** There is hope for our industry on the horizon.

Be positive and hey, like Addi always says, "Have fun!"
Amanda
@amandagram12
Originally from Saugus, MA

Dear Cameron,

When the lights are bright again you will weep tears of joy. This year has been so challenging and yet so rewarding. I've always been a person who prides themself on having many other interests other than theatre. I love books, I love food and wine and cooking. And I love DOGS! Any and every dog. I never wanted my career to be my identity. Don't get me wrong, I love what I do. **But what I do does not define me.** I was 3 previews in for a new Broadway show and exhausted when the shutdown happened. I was slightly relieved for a few weeks off. My boyfriend and I were moving apartments while both in tech and previews for new shows and the time off was very helpful. And then we quickly realized this time off was going to be much longer than a few weeks. It took a while to wrap my head around it all and my immediate response was to shut down and shut off. I deleted my public Instagram and didn't really want to reach out and discuss it all with my peers. **I needed space. And I took it.** I don't regret that for a minute but the longing set in and I missed my community and my job and my day to day life. I love what I do, and I've always known that, but this year really reminded me how MUCH I love it. This community is unlike any other and all of us who are lucky enough to work in the theatre industry know that. Whether it is community theatre, regional theatre, off Broadway or Broadway. Special people gravitate there. And tough, resilient people. I am proud to say that Broadway is a part of who I am and I will be weeping when the overture plays the downbeat of our first performance back, whenever that may be. Just as I am weeping writing this letter.

With so much love to my beautiful community, I miss you.

Truly miss you.
Cameron
@Cameron.nyc

Dear Jeannie,

When the Lights are bright again, I must choose.

This year has been far from a lost one. I feel as though I have moved restlessly through the Kubler-Ross 5 stages of grief while still holding onto the tail end of hope that dips and flies and circles around the return of our industry.

Rumors, media, science, politicians...what and whom to believe?

I lean towards science and my own parsing of the other three.

Back on March 12, 2020...that already most difficult of years, when we were told we all needed to go home, take our things...a few weeks, a month, perhaps a bit more?

An usher had gotten ill, *Moulin Rouge* had canceled a matinee. Soon followed the Broadway Shutdown in a business that can be as predictable and dependable as a Swiss watch.

I had been in previews on *Company*, the reimagined revival helmed by Marianne Elliott. I was dressing Patti LuPone. On a LOA from *Hamilton* at The Rodgers.

Suddenly, no fan line at the stage door. No gathering. We wondered at work the next day if we would be sent home. Surely not, but shouldn't we be?

After years of working long hours six days a week, 8 shows a week, it took quite a while to learn to let go of the feeling that I had somewhere I was supposed to be. There weren't buses to catch. Hard to stop my internal hamster wheel.

To suddenly not have your "purpose." Thrust back into home life, where I was never the one making dinner, doing bedtime. I was a stranger in my own home. They had to adjust to me being places I normally wouldn't be. Shaking things up.

I am still reacquainting myself with my daughter, my husband.

I dove into political action, into mask making, into trying to help my union by creating an online craft fair. We always had live ones in some theatre's green room around the holidays and marveled at each other's hidden talents...Unbelievable that it was now the holiday season and we were still unemployed.

Friends, young friends got it. Some died. Astonishing. Shocking. Unreal.

The powers in Washington didn't seem interested in getting on top of it. Despair. Loss...of purpose, employment, place, identity?

> The **deliciousness of a morning** without a bus to catch midday.

It's a new virus. We are still learning. The frontier of such a wildly unpredictable fiend. In one person, few symptoms, in another, clotting, neuroses, organ failure, respiratory distress, death.

Haunted frontline workers. Scared cashiers.

A divided nation that seemed to forget what "we are all in this together" means. Ignorance and fear and bigotry into the sunlight.

And here I am. More than a year later.

Strangely, to me at least, I am both excited and nervous thinking about the return. Broadway will return. No doubt in my mind. But do I want to go back? And if I do, will it feel the same? Can it?

In some warped way, what I always wanted was that extra day off, the nights to see my daughter after school. To see friends. To take that vacation. To have "a life."

Well, we have little money to take the vacation but I have the days, the time.

Will what satisfied me before still satisfy me now? Now that I have been reminded of what a weekend is? Of what watching my child grow means. Of being able to see my husband's online Zoom production without taking a night off?

The deliciousness of a morning without a bus to catch midday.

To come home in daylight and leisurely make dinner. The talk at dinner. Time to pursue that hobby.

To spring clean over the course of a week, not on a Monday.

How quiet the streets in the suburbs are. Traffic is picking back up...it makes me nervous.

For all that we have been through, the journey back and the possibility that not much will have changed is a little terrifying to me. PTSD? Perhaps.

Or the thought that I've RE prioritized my life during this enforced hiatus. I have no doubt that art matters more than ever. No doubt. We need the mirror on humanity, the catharsis, the laughter, the recognition, the joy! The camaraderie, the roar of that crowd...

Will I be satisfied with my place in it after having seen all that I missed?

If I am being honest I would have to say...

I really don't know.

Onward!
Jeannie
@jeannie.naughton
Originally from Bronx, NY

Dear Aaron,

When the lights are bright again, how much will you miss turning hers off at bedtime? Will your dresser helping you into your costume feel as nice as helping her into pajamas around that same time of night? Can a curtain call warm your heart as much as that little kiss on the cheek, just before she crawls off to bed?

I don't know how you were ever able to be away 5 nights a week. You've been a dad longer than a Broadway actor. But then again, you've been an actor almost always. It is an essential facet of your identity. So these many months, as we've lived our longest without stepping onstage, other facets have needfully, rightfully, risen to the top. Aaron the dad has become your main role, and how you've grown in it.

You are Aaron the dad, and Aaron the actor. He is you and you are him. Both make each other better. So when the lights are bright again, you be there when she turns hers on. Help her out of her pjs and into a cozy hoodie to greet that crisp morning air you both adore. A kiss on the cheek is nice in the morning, too.

Inlustret lumine,
Aaron
@aaronbartz
Originally from Great Falls, MT

Dear Colin,

When the lights are bright again will you have cleaned your computer screen? Will you have safely delivered your second baby blanket you made and will you have been able to hold sweet Naya upon the delivery? Will you have lost someone closer to you? Will your friend's lungs get him through the show or will his knee take the pain crown? Will you have purchased a kayak? Will Breonna Taylor have had her justice? Will your back still cause you pain from lack of physical movement or will your body ache because you have jumped back into 8 shows a week? Will one be of preference? Will your skin still fire up and peel? Will you have embraced gin? Will Pangea have survived? Will there have emerged a midtown bar that embraces the joys, dramatics and dangers of the Broadway community? Will the self-polarization of uptown and downtown have finally disappeared? Will you have taken a ballet class at home? Will you have written a song? Will you aim to speak? Will you triumph over the fear of lack of intelligence in the workspace? Will you have made a bow and arrow or did you purchase it? Will you have let your cat Rambo become an outdoor cat and if so, has he survived the eagles? Will you have watched Citizen Kane?

Sincerely and with Love,
Colin
@Colin_Hollis_Shannon
Originally from Barryville, NY

Dear Kyle,

When the lights are bright again your inner light will shine brighter than ever before. This past year has been quite a journey filled with many challenges. I was living the life I had dreamt of since I was 5 years old when all of a sudden the world stopped. The career I had worked so hard to build suddenly got washed away and what was left? An emptiness. A vast emptiness where a bunch of questions were unearthed. Who am I without this? I'd like to think that I'm a well rounded individual but like many others who find themselves in this crazy theatre world which requires so much of ourselves (dare I say 100%) I was discovering that without my job I wasn't sure who I was. I had let my career define me and in doing so forgot about me. This led to many months of some deep soul searching and in the end self discovery. Rebirth. Had I not had this break… this pause… then I would have never had to sit with these unsettling questions and do the work required to find peace. Find true joy… Happiness. As hard as this year has been I will forever be grateful for the time I was given to discover all the wonderful things that make up me, that actually have nothing to do with my career. My love for baking… my love of dogs…. how madly in love with my partner I am, the joy I feel dancing with no 8 count, but most of all the importance of taking time to sit back and just be at home with myself in the present moment. Not worry about that job I didn't get or what show I want to do next. Just be. Alive. Right now. In this very moment. Breathe. You are enough.

I love you,
Kyle
@kylebrown_85

KYLE BROWN
Originally from
Amsterdam, NY

Dear Nick,

When the lights are bright again I won't go back to the version of myself that existed. I've learned too much from this forced perspective to retrogress to a now outdated operating system. I've been unemployed for long stints in my career but never without the overwhelming attitude that I was falling behind or losing time. But now, a complete stop in solidarity? No weight of feeling less than my peers or than the expectations I put onto myself. The gift to come out of this time has been a chance to sit with my life. BE with myself. With my partner. With our animal. Look outward at what is happening outside of my career. The blessings that exist all around me and also the injustices that make my egocentric career path look so small. Look inward at who I am at 37. Who I really am without running toward a goal or trying to be what someone wants me to be. Remembering why I run that race in the first place. Why I love it so much. The joy that radiates within me and explodes out when I'm completely present. It has given me space and time to sit with who I am, reconnect and rediscover that person. I remembered what makes me unique. I remembered I don't need to please everyone else but myself. Success doesn't need to be measured by credits or money or fame. A rebirth of gratitude came from allowing the software update of my soul and accepting who I am without the approval of others. I can see that I was seeking validation externally for far too long and stop that noise. I will be better for it. My art will be better. My relationships will be deeper. I will cry harder and laugh louder. I can't go back to Nick Adams from 2020 because that person no longer exists. There is only me here today. Now. When the lights are bright again I will continue to live in this vibration. I can only move forward. I can't control the storm but I've better learned how to steer the ship and why I'm sailing it in the first place.

You can and you will,
Nick Adams
@thenickadams

NICK ADAMS
Originally from
Erie, PA

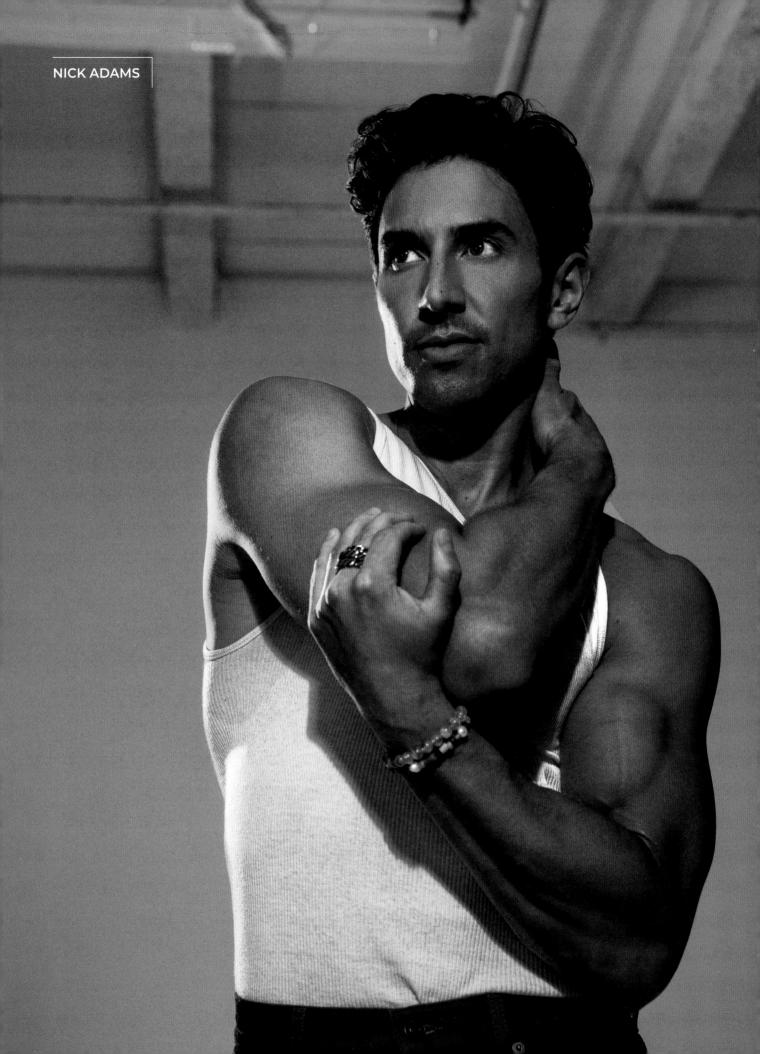

NICK ADAMS

Dear Erica,

When the lights are bright again, you will be called to duty. A duty to brighten the lights for everyone coming out of this dark time. When the lights are bright again, you will be lucky enough to be given a chance to breathe love into a community that has been wounded. When the lights are bright again, you will be welcomed home, Erica. As you look into the windows of the souls of your community you will all have the understanding that you have had a detour from the world you once knew. **You will all be different, because the world stopped, yet everything happened.** Everyone will have lost something or someone. Everyone will have had moments of darkness just as you had. This will now be your time to help build new roads that lead to a kinder world. A world that is awakened, yet needs a giant hug. Do it with your art. Be the bright light, and use your first love as a vessel. There is nothing like your first love, the theatre, and the family you have within it. This wounded world needs you, and this is your time to help heal it. You have now learned how precious time is and how you couldn't get enough of it even when the world stopped. **Never forget the gift of the time that you have had with your loved ones, and perform for those who were robbed of time with theirs. Always remember that everyone deserves for the lights to be bright again.** When you come back and witness the smiles and the tears of your peers, hear your half hour call, listen to the downbeat of the orchestra, and take in your first moment back on the stage, do it for those who can't. Do it for those who didn't get the time they deserved. When you take your bow, hold the hand of your beloved cast member, Doreen Montalvo, and all of those whose lights have permanently dimmed since you last walked out of the stage door of the Sondheim Theatre. Most importantly, as your mother always says, "enjoy the moment" because all we have are moments until our light goes out.

Your loving self,
Erica
@ericamansfieldny
Originally born in France,
raised in Houston, TX

> ## Do it for those who didn't get the **time** they deserved.

Dear Barrett,

When the lights are bright again, I hope they re-energize you and reconnect you with your passion…performing. I know you are considering the possibility that it may not- and that's OK. You have been so fortunate to have had a successful career doing something that you love for over 20 years. However, you have also been so fortunate in the past year to discover **new loves and new passions**. Also, you were given the most wonderful gift of time. Time to spend with your son, your family, and yourself. It may not have been the most ideal time, and it certainly was quite DARK at times. But, I hope that time gives you a clearer understanding of what you hope to get out of the next Act of your life. When the lights are bright again, you may squint and want to retreat. You might run to their warmth. If you're lucky, you may even feel like it's the first time again. Indeed, returning to work will be challenging, frustrating, exciting, and full of anxiety. Luckily, you will experience all of it along with the rest of your family and your community. Don't let any self-doubt take charge. Relish the moments, the people, and the process of getting the lights back on. Then, let your eyes adjust before you jump to any conclusions. The stage is a magical place and I hope it provides you with more magic in your life as well as a means to support your family.

Hopefully, that passion is still there…
and if it isn't…
take another bow, smile, and exit stage right.
Barrett
@barrettmartinnyc
Originally from Chicago, IL

GRIEF

Dear Heather,

When the lights are bright again I still won't have a baby. People say women have children in their 40's all the time. What they don't say, is how physically hard, emotionally difficult, anxiety ridden, and expensive it is to actually achieve. I had never wanted a child. Performing had been my child. I loved it unconditionally and sacrificed everything for it. It puked and pooped all over me, but I would just wipe myself off and love it even more…until I met Matt. We got married the week after I turned 40, and we wanted a baby together.

Our first miscarriage happened 7 months later in January 2019. 5 weeks prior, I had been offered a temporary replacement track in *Anastasia* on Broadway… but I had also found out I was 7 weeks pregnant. At that time, I "fit the costume," but wasn't sure if it would still fit 2 months later at the start of my contract. No precedent on how to handle that one…a long Google search only showed info about performers who currently had children or the pregnancies of Broadway stars Audra Mcdonald and Kelly O'Hara who were already starring in shows when they got pregnant. For fear of being black balled, I gracefully backed out.

I ended up playing Velma Kelly in a production of Chicago instead. On our day off during tech week, I drove back to the city for my 12 week ultrasound. 30 seconds after she had started swiping the wand over my stomach, the flustered technician quickly and silently left to get the doctor. My husband and I were left in the exam room with the lights off staring at a too still image of our tiny child on the screen.

The fetus had to be surgically removed by D&C. As per my request, our director for Chicago told the company I was gone to have a "procedure." The day I came back, we teched the opening of Act 2.

My first words on stage after losing my child were:

"She says she's gonna have a baby…now why didn't I think of that?"

Performing was no longer my child. I had lost my child.

> ## "Performing had been my child. I loved it unconditionally and sacrificed everything for it."

But I was only 40…I had plenty of time…according to the "people."

The next year became a blur of IVF fertility treatments, doctors, nurses, needles, injections, retrievals, many people I didn't know looking at my vagina, and so much waiting… waiting for what ended up being disappointment after disappointment. Then, the world met "Rona," and was catapulted into a global pandemic…and it all stopped. Trying to get pregnant had been my job. And just like everyone else…I lost my job.

Like so many couples with pandemic time on their hands, Matt and I tried naturally. Pregnancy sex has its pluses and minuses, but it becomes more about the result than the experience. Twisting the knife in my heart were the constant social media pregnancy announcements for their "Covid Babies." "Oops…we got pregnant;" "Look what we did during a pandemic?!" Ahhh!!!

Sure, a year later I have acquired new cooking skills, I can edit videos like a pro, I knit lightning fast, I am a phenom on a jetski, I cut my family's hair, I became BFFs with my parents, I can self-tape like a champ, and my husband and I have deepened our relationship to a level of sheer laughter, but I still don't have a baby.

In the fall, of 2020, when the world was in the infancy stages of re-opening, we went to a new fertility clinic. More doctors, needles, injections, retrievals, and money…I still don't have a baby. During the 2020 Christmas holidays, Matt and I escaped to the Poconos with a couple bottles of tequila and zero fucks. We conceived. We had zero idea.

On January 15th 2021, the day of my preliminary blood-

> **These are the moments to grow stronger and become a fighter.** So thats what you're going to do. You are going to continue fighting and hoping for better and brighter days ahead.

work for my 6th round of IVF; 2 years to the day that I found out about the first miscarriage; the doctor called and told me I was pregnant! He gave us the IVF baby pregnancy treatment which treated us to weekly ultrasounds to track the baby's progress. Week 7 we saw the tiny little heart flutter. Week 8, we heard a loud and healthy heartbeat. Week 9, stillness and quiet. Matt and I held hands silently in the cold cab ride home. The D&C removal was scheduled for the following day. I had lost another child, just 3 months before my 43rd birthday.

I wish the next step was to simply keep plugging away and go for a 6th round of IVF, but my hormone levels did not return to normal post fetal removal. I apparently had what is called a Partial Molar Pregnancy which left my uterus with a mass of small pre-cancerous tumors. I had another surgery to remove the tissue. I now have to undergo a form of chemotherapy treatments to reset my pregnancy hormone levels, and due to the complications from the treatments, I can't even try to get pregnant for almost a year from now. I will then be almost 44 years old, and I still won't have a baby.

I don't know how the next few months or year will play out. Even when the lights are bright again and allows my shadow to grace backdrops again, it will possess a melancholy from the losses and disappointments. The song and dance will have more depth and the human connection will be more genuine, but I still won't have a baby.

Heather
@heatherparcells
Originally from Newport News, VA

Dear Gabriella,

When the lights are bright again, you will finally be back home. This time of stillness has definitely brought on its challenges emotionally, mentally, and spiritually. You have had to evaluate life and ask the question: what is my life like without the theatre and the arts? Its been difficult to navigate that through this time because it is so much of who you are—being an artist, performer, teacher, and creator. You wake up everyday wanting to go out into the world and get to do what you were born to do and instead if feels like groundhog day. You sit around and are waiting for that phone to ring or for word that something is going to change. You have had to lose people during this pandemic and feel the pain and grief of them being gone. Just feels like so much all at once. Sometimes you want to scream and cry and at other times you just want to stay quiet and alone. But I know there is that light inside you that still believes—believes that this won't be forever. This is just a moment in time in your life that you have to fight through and push through. **These are the moments to grow stronger and become a fighter.** So thats what you're going to do. You are going to continue fighting and hoping for better and brighter days ahead. The day will come when music will be blaring from the theater's and cheers will be heard from the crowds. That will be a special day. So keep reminding yourself, this is only intermission and we will back again better and stronger than ever.

Holding onto hope,
Xoxo
Gabriella
Originally from New York, NY

Dear Jake,

When the lights are bright again, I am so afraid I won't be there to celebrate with my cast family. When the lights went dark I was playing 12 year old Christopher Hillard in *Doubtfire the Musical*. I am now 14 years old. I have grown 4 inches since Broadway shut down and my voice has dropped. For a child actor that is basically the kiss of death. The producer and director have let me know they want me back. But even I realize this has gone on way too long. No one knew this could shut down Broadway for a year!!!! I am not mad. Well, I am mad. But not at anyone. I am mainly sad. I love performing on stage. And this cast was amazing. Not just talent. This cast is amazing people. And I miss them all so much. I just want to be there on that first day and hug and cry with everyone. That's what makes me sad the most. The thought of not being there to hug everyone and realize we made it. We got through this horrible period in our life. And honestly, I was so proud of myself for originating my second Broadway role in three years. And I know that is the selfish part of me. And I will get over it. But it will always sting I think.

> **I am mainly sad.** I love performing on stage.

But most of all I just want *Doubtfire* to live on. It is an amazing show. Rob McClure is incredible. He deserves the Tony. The Tony was just sitting there waiting for him before the shutdown. Even if I can't be there the worst thing that could ever happen would be for this show not to survive. But, I am certain it will. It is beautiful and will only be more amazing after the long wait.

I am trying to protect my heart and move on. But it is hard to move on from these wonderful people and this amazing show. But deep down I am hope I am there when the lights go back on.

Holding onto hope,
Jake
@jake_ryan_flynn
Originally from Wenham, MA

Dear Martin,

When the lights are bright again, I hope you never lose your purpose. I hope you know that hard work does pay off. I hope you know that you are loved, enough, and that it is important to be you. I hope you remember the three things that one of your best friends told you to remember, which is **"I'm proud, I'm thankful, and I deserve it."** I hope you know that it says something about you and your abilities and who you are that a couple of your idols know who you are and love you. I hope you know you aren't a fool and that all you need is love, like John and Paul said. I hope you know that you're a true song and dance man who brings people joy. I hope you know that a ton of people love you and care about you. I know that losing Aunt Mary Lou was the hardest thing you have had to deal with, but know that you gained the best angel in your life. Don't doubt yourself. You are here for a reason.

Love,
Martin
@martinotheshowman
Originally from New York, NY

Dear Phoen,

When the lights are bright again I hope you'll be able to have a better time in life! To meet more people and be nicer than you were ever before the quarantine.

Please know you are loved even if you go through difficulties in life. For example, the Shadow Self workbook is bearing down, but when you had to figure it out you were not having a good day so let it rest I guess. You will REALLY go through times people won't understand, they will make your blood boil (like crazy sometimes!) and you won't get your way. It's okay to feel disappointed and struggle, but life is a joke and everything IS a fraud regardless so think of it that way. Yes.

Stay safe at home and keep annoying your cat. He will come out as better too. Just pull through cause God will be there when the lights are bright again.

Holding onto Him,
Phoen
@ellemusika
Originally from Manila

Dear Eleri,

When the lights are bright again, I'm going to take the many lessons I've learned throughout this pandemic and apply them to a healthier mindset to take with me to every audition, callback, performance, etc. And with that being said, I won't go to every single audition that I can possibly go to. I won't guilt myself for not going to every single audition possible either. I won't think about what the people behind the table want; I will just be. I will have grieved the losses that this time has brought me, like a relationship that was going really well, but had to end because of unrelated outside forces. But I know we're meant to be together so I will continue to look forward to our rekindling of our flame, even if looking back on our past hurts at times. **I will move forward into a world where absolutes are no longer and emotional and mental fluidity is celebrated and taken care of.** Where I don't need to feel guilty for not wanting to take in any theater at all because I now know who I am without the white knuckled need of the labels that "theater" and "actor" gave me for so long. I am not my occupation, but rather my occupation is a part of me. Like a rectangle is a square, but a square is not a rectangle, my art is a part of me, but I am not my art. So it's okay to take time away from it and it's also okay to be completely and utterly enveloped in it too. Those extremes exist within me and I will go on to be a lot less judgemental of their coexistence. I will be a better person to myself and therefore a better artist.

Holding on to hope,
Eleri
@eleriward
Originally from Chicago, IL

> I will just be.

> Those waves of sadness which have threatened to take you too will wane and you will find your footing again.

Dear Tiffany,

When the lights are bright again you will be there. Yes, Tabitha will still be gone, lost like so many this past year. You will be grateful for the time that you got to spend with her when the world shut down and for the time you were able to grieve her loss. Those waves of sadness which have threatened to take you too will wane and you will find your footing again. How lucky. How blessed. As a twin you have never gone through big moments in life alone. **How fitting even in your grief the world is grieving with you.** Your personal devastating loss is shared with a global sense of loss and love and community. Your love of theater too is based in the collaborative effort of many to share personal and yet universal stories with the world. So when the lights are bright again you will continue writing, and performing, and promoting works as you did before. Don't stop living and loving and enjoying your life. **Those we have lost won't return to us and it gives them no joy to see us refusing to live.** When the lights are bright again, you too can be bright!

Shine, my love
Tiffany
@Tiffanyimcc
Originally from O'Fallon, MO

" **Be Thankful** for the good,
the bad, and the ugly. "

Dear MiMi,

When the lights are bright again you will be so happy you wrote this letter.

You ran from writing this because you're caught behind the fog. The fog of fear, anxiety, loss, and pure sadness that this year has brought you. Right now you're scared to walk through it. You know there is another side. You know it doesn't go on forever. You just have to take the first step.

But today the sun is shining into your apartment and you're sitting in gratitude for the beautiful things that God has brought into your life in this transitional time. So you thought, no more running let's write.

When those lights are bright again MiMi, you will feel at home. You will have stopped running through the maze of doubt and come through on the other side more certain than ever that performing is not what you do it is WHO YOU ARE. Performing is what feeds you. Performing is your light through the darkness. THAT IS OK. THAT IS BEAUTIFUL. THAT IS MAGICAL.

To know your calling and follow it with conviction is for the brave. Throughout this awful pandemic, though you may have questioned it, you were brave. You saw this end goal and you knew your place was on that stage. Do not flush away the dark moments from the past. **Honor them. Honor the feelings.** For we cannot have the light if we do not make it through the dark. You made it through and I am proud of you.

I hope you take a moment each day and stand on that stage and thank God for every bit of it. Every hard step. Every hard day. Every correction. Every costume and costumer. Every stage manager. Every friend. Every colleague. Every dance class with friends. Every postshow hug and celebration. Every person that helps and uplifts you every day. Be Thankful for the good, the bad, and the ugly.

Take a moment to feel the glitter pulsing around and inside your heart for it has been building and building, and it is ready to take on this new world.

I love you. Again, I am so proud of you.

Spread Your Glitter!
MiMi
@mimidulla

Dear B,

When the lights are bright again, how will you even look up?

I'm so angry. I'm angry that I see my own profession as non-essential, even frivolous. I look at old, peeling subway posters for Broadway shows on my commute to my temporary job at a COVID testing site, and I'm angry. I'm angry that I was so excited for something that the world has deemed unnecessary. I'm angry that I was ever excited for something so impractical, as people die by the thousands every day.

I'm angry at friends who have somehow found the will to stay creative. Some have released albums, filmed, choreographed, or found new artistic paths. I haven't sung in over a year, except for humming in the shower, and honestly, my shower sessions could use a vocal coach. I used to be proud of my accomplishments, but they feel meaningless now. Were they ever worth anything to begin with?

I'm angry at "jokes about out of work actors." Like we're all a bunch of ridiculous people, and it's a laugh to think of us trying to cope. Like we won't be able to pay our rent, and will try to cover expenses with a tap dance, or singing for our supper. It's not funny. My career was deleted. And I worked hard for it. It never offered me security or benefits, and I still made a living out of it. **That took work.**

I'm angry at everyone who can see the light at the end of the tunnel that I just can't see.

I'm angry at how dramatic this sounds. Some friends booked their first Broadway contracts when theaters shuttered. Some lost family members, and couldn't even have funerals. What's my pain compared to that? Nothing. And I'm angry at myself for even feeling it.

I'm trying to just keep going—one day at a time, one foot in front of the other. Even if it feels like walking blindly into the dark. But I'm afraid that, when the lights are bright again, everyone else will be ready. Everyone but me.

Well, good luck,
B
@rmasonwygal
Originally from Bellflower, CA

Dear Zach,

When the lights are bright again, that first bow is for you.

When you were younger your comfort zone and adventurous zone were practically one and the same. You were a wild child, life of the party, unafraid, and always game to try something new. But as you grew older that became less and less the case. I began denying you countless opportunities— artistically, socially, financially, recreationally, you name it. Adventurous and risky and new were no longer comfortable. I got so good at convincing you we were not credible enough, worthy enough, or talented enough that we stopped trying altogether. Your comfort and adventurous zones were shrinking, and I was so much to blame.

This year has allowed me to recognize exactly how much we were going through the motions. We'd put on a smile, sign in at the callboard, and get through our show, **but there was so much more beneath the surface**. The pandemic helped us face our deepest stressors, traumas, and anxieties—all of which pushed me into convincing you to live and think small in the first place. I'm so grateful this year let me rediscover you, what you truly want, and how we can find comfort in the fear.

> **You are grounded. You are connected. You are ready.**

You're saying, "Yes!" to so much more these days, and while absolutely terrifying it's quite thrilling, too. You are grounded. You are connected. You are ready. Ultimately, we are all more capable and deserving than we allow ourselves to be, and I'm glad the time since Broadway shut down has helped us understand that.

When the lights are bright again, we will be, too.

I love you,
Zach
@aspiredance
Originally from Bloomingdale, IL

Dear Diamond,

When the lights are bright again it won't be the same. It'll be exciting, it'll be emotional, it'll be joyous, and it will be something that you never take for granted again but it won't be the same. It will be a reminder of everything that you've survived as well as everything that you've lost. It won't be the same without the loved ones that you've lost. It won't be the same performing to an audience that is missing the one person who was your biggest supporter who you'd want, more that anything, to be there. Let it encourage you though, let it be a beacon of hope for you, and let it tell you that regardless of all the terrible things that happened, you were fortunate enough to see the lights come back on and be in the lights. **Theatre is resilient**, that's why you love it so much, and so are you! Smile when the lights come back on and bask in them and enjoy them as long as you live!

Love,
Diamond
@diamondessencewhite

Dear Caitlin,

When the lights are bright again you will hopefully feel free. I have been trapped in this weird alternate universe. A constant fog. I have spent many sleepless nights feeling heartbroken, lost, confused, scared, and angry for all the pain our world is carrying. I went from working and building my career in the city of my dreams, to finding myself in my childhood home for months at 27. There was a weird guilt and ache in me like I abandoned my city as it went through the darkness of that time. **I went from singing every day to not being able to hum a tune.** I was too scared to sing. Scared of what it would bring out in me and the pain I would feel doing something that reminded me of what so many of us just lost. I can't wait for the lights to be bright again. There is so much that needs to be rebuilt in our industry and I am hopeful we can see real change. I'm also terrified. It is hard not to feel behind in this industry. There are people established in this business, and rightfully so, that will be able to get back to their next project or to the Broadway show/tour they were doing prior. I am still working on finding an agent, getting casting directors to know my name, building my resume, life, and connections here. I am scared the momentum I have gained hustling over the past few years will be gone. But the perspective, knowledge, learning, unlearning, and fire within me that I have gained this past year has made me know myself more than ever. When the lights are bright again I WILL be free. I will be full of so much gratitude to do what I love again that I won't care as much what the person behind the table thinks of me. This past year has been a huge reminder how precious life is and to use the gifts God gave us. I am done apologizing for who I am and letting people make me question my worth. Those first 16 bars back will only be for me. I feel more free just thinking about it. I love you my strong, resilient, beautiful community. I can't wait to be under the lights with you again and for the beautiful overtures to be heard all around the world.

All my love and light,
Caitlin
@cndoak
Originally from Gainesville, FL

Dear Candelle,

When the lights are bright again, more than a year will have passed since the last time I sat in a theater. As I heard the reports of just two weeks and we'll be back I was hopeful for the shows I had bought tickets to for later on the following month. But as shows were canceling performances, pushing back opening my shining light was dimming.

You don't want to set all of your joy into one capsule. It should be spread. But a major part of my time was spent seeing shows. Enjoying walking around Times Square. Peaceful trips to the museum. And so quickly everything went away. The year has been very hard to find the same passion that theater brought. Zoom concerts aren't personal. They don't have the same connection. It's been a very hard year without any type of live entertainment.

Do I miss theater? Very much so! But not having it has made me appreciate the memories that I will cherish so much. Every blurry stage door selfie. Live concerts that brought on a special guest that you were not expecting to see. The conversations you get from actors signing your Playbill. Reading your Playbill and the lights dim and the overture starts. I will not take anything for granted when the light return. This year has made me think about the song "Where The Lost Things Go" from *Mary Poppins Returns*. The line "Nothing's gone forever/ Only out of place" I am looking forward to intermission being over soon. I know when it is, it will return brighter than ever and help return the shine for those who need it!

Shine Bright Always,
Candelle
@cmonteagudo89
Originally from Staten Island, NY

Dear Stefanie,

When the lights are bright again, yours will be too.

In the deepest part of you, the day-to-day feels lost - I know, you miss it.

You miss the challenge of being your truest self in front of a table of strangers. Or friends. You miss blowing it. You miss nailing the f*%k outta it. You miss spotting girls on the subway in full beat with three meals, a snack, two changes of clothes, and a curling iron sticking out of their backpack. At 6am. You miss hoping for the callback. You miss hoping for the job. You miss prepping 10+ pages for callbacks the next day and doing one page from a different packet instead. You miss Hells Kitchen at dusk, crowds of people bustling from Juniors' to whichever theatre they were headed to (probably *The Lion King*). You miss the buzz when the house lights dim. You miss hearing the cheers at stage doors while walking to the subway afterwards. You miss smiles and knowing glances with actors in ball caps "in the wild" on two-show days. You miss your friends' Broadway debuts. You miss the option of dreaming about yours.

Okay, okay, listen - I know what you're thinking. "Yeah it'll all be back someday - but the annoying things will be annoying, and the frustrating things will be frustrating, and we'll complain about all the things we complained about before, even when the lights are bright again." And maybe you're right. **But maybe, just maybe, we'll love those things a little more, now that we've lived without them.**

For now, the marquees are dimmed tombstones in some sort of sacred graveyard where the smattering of tourists wander aloof taking pictures and eating bad pretzels, and you want to scream at them,

"THIS ISN'T IT. THIS ISN'T NEW YORK.

YOU SHOULDN'T BE HERE, NOT LIKE THIS.

WE ARE GRIEVING."

Deep down, Stef, you know. If they wander aloof now, they'll be here when the grieving's through. And you know - when the lights are bright again, yours will be, too.

Soon,
Stefanie
@pocketfulofierce
Originally from New York, NY

Dear Lisa,

When the lights are bright again, I'm not sure what the world will look like, but I do know it will need live theater, music and dance.

To be asked to write about this past year is complicated. Not just because at the time I'm writing this, we are still in the pandemic and live entertainment is still dark. Not just because my grandfather passed away, without my getting to be with my family. Not just because someone who was once my best friend was lost to the virus and I was never able to say goodbye to him. Not just because of how difficult it is trying to work through profound grief while totally isolated from family and friends. **You simply never realize how much you need your grief acknowledged and need a hug until you don't have one.** Not just because I haven't seen my family in person in over 16 months and counting. Not just because the world as a whole is suffering an equally unimaginable traumatic experience. In a word, this past year has been brutal.

But, man am I lucky. To still be here, living and working in the greatest city in the world ... and still be sane. Due in no small part to an army of people who I love deeply. My family who FaceTime with me multiple times a day, every single day of this pandemic. I wouldn't have survived any of it without them. My friends who check in constantly, even if it's only to say I love you. My clients who found a way to keep working and in turn, kept me working. I have a small army of people who I love, who love me back, and for that I'm extremely lucky.

If I'm being totally honest, I'm not taking anything new out of this. I think I've always been a survivor and I've always known that I wouldn't be that person if it wasn't for my relationships. I believe that relationships are everything in life. It's never something I've taken for granted. And the relationship live theater has with the world may be one of the last to come back in person, but it will be the most important. Our souls are nothing without our relationship to the arts. The world will not take that for granted. I predict that as soon as it's safe to do so, live entertainment will be back bigger than it ever was and I can not wait to cheer on my friends and clients while complaining about the person sitting next to me.

Stay safe. Be patient. We will get through this and we will be back on stage again.

Love,
Lisa
@lisagoldbergpr
Originally from South Carolina

Dear Unhoused Usher,

When the lights are bright again ...
Like Elphaba without Glinda,
Like Bialystock without Bloom,
Life without your ushering gig
Feels akin to doom and gloom.

Like Pippin without a corner,
Like Dorothy in Oz,
Your world without live theater
Has you feeling oh, so lost!

So as Tony yearns for Maria,
As Porgy yearns for Bess,
We yearn the lights go bright again
When we beat this COVID mess!

Have faith, the best of times are near,
No need to fret, my dear.
With hope and heart and spirits high,
We patiently persevere!

Yours 'Til Curtain's Up,
Unhoused Usher
@joanne_serpico_mieszkowski
Originally from East Brunswick, NJ

> "Our souls are nothing without our **relationship to the arts.** The world will not take that for granted."

JUSTICE

Dear New To NYC,

When the lights are bright again, you have a responsibility to do better. As you continue to break slowly into the commercial theatrical scene, you need to be an ally, an activist, a speaker, a listener, a learner. You need to continue to open your lens to the world outside of your own body. You need to be part of the active change that needs to happen throughout the Broadway community. Sitting back and allowing yourself to be subconsciously content with–and unaware of–the white patriarchy is no longer tolerable. **Be an amplifier of Black artists.** When put into positions of hiring power, use that power to intentionally diversify. Push forward. Do better. Don't stop.

With that, when the lights are bright again, continue to never take an ounce of creativity, employment, or even being an audience member for granted. You are so privileged to be doing what you love for a living! Post-pandemic, every smile, every long day of rehearsal, every moment of boiling stress, every laugh, and every inspiration should bring you nothing but joy. Your sense of purpose, enthusiasm, and connection will return. I can't wait to see you genuinely smile again. **The world needs it just as much as you crave it.**

Get ready for an explosion–**a Renaissance**–of artistry and activism that will define the rest of your time in the theatrical world. Be gracious. Be better. Be inspirational. Be inspired. Just be.

Holding on to hope,
New To NYC
Originally from Sewell, NJ

Dear Cris Eli Blak,

When the lights are bright again let's hope that they shine on different kinds of stages. Let those stages be occupied by people who look like this country, who sound like this country. So many stories have changed in the last year, so many people have lost and so many people have grown. We have all changed and with those changes must come a change of look in our theatres. Let the little brown boy know that he can be the next Norm Lewis. Let the little brown girl know that her voice is more than joyful noise. Let her know it is art. **Let them know that they are a part of a community where inclusivity is not a trend, but a trait that will be passed on from one generation to the next, only improving.** When the lights are bright again, let the doors open too. And let those doors be large and wide, allowing as many people from as many neighborhoods, blocks and boroughs to walk onto the stage and realize the potential that our chosen art has in this world. Holding onto hope, holding hope in my heart.

I'll see you under the spotlight.

With love,
Cris Eli Blak
@criseliblak
Originally from Louisville, KY

> "Push forward. Do better. Don't stop."

Dear Hallie,

When the lights are bright again, take your bubble with you. Meditate. Dream bigger than you thought possible. Hug people. Breathe. When the lights are bright again, love yourself, even as the world reflects back to you what it thinks you should be. Ask for things. **Fight** on behalf of others and the world you want to live in, not just for the best version of the world we already have. Enjoy singing. Listen to children. Call your parents.

> **"There's no stronger wind than the one that blows down a lonesome railroad line**
>
> **No prettier sight than lookin' back on a town you left behind**
>
> **There is nothin' that's as real as a love that's in my mind**
>
> **Close your eyes**
> **I'll be here in the morning**
> **Close your eyes**
> **I'll be here for a while"**
>
> **–Townes Van Zandt**

Love,
Your peaceful self
@hbinsane
Originally from New York, NY

> " What do you do when you finally learn and realize what it means, what it feels like, to have Blackness as your superpower? "

Dear Lala,

When the lights are bright again. When the lights are finally bright again? Wow. I don't know. What do you say about the past year+?

When the lights are bright again you will have been part of this history. Living history. Lived through the turmoil, the reckoning, of an artist's worst nightmare: no access to the thing that we, you and I, have identified our whole life as the thing we were born to do. What we thought was our superpower.

What do you do without that? What do you do when there's nothing but time to think about your life? And your choices. And your career 'before.' When there's nothing to do but wait.

And then, you'll remember immediately and forever, when George Floyd and Breonna Taylor died, and the world broke open, and we were reminded of Trayvon Martin, and Emmett Till, and then we, you and I, were finally allowed to see what our real nightmare entailed. All that time, all that waiting, all that thinking, was so we could have space to become our true self. **To see the world for what it was. To see that we've been lied to about our superpower.**

What do you do when you finally learn and realize what it means, what it feels like, to have Blackness as your superpower? What do you do when there's finally space to say "no" to things? To everything?

What did you do?

When the lights are bright again, I won't forget. There's so much more to life than the stage. And the lights. But, my goodness, you and I both know that that's what makes live theatre so truly precious.

I friggin love the lights. I missed them. And gosh I missed you.

Here's to always growing. Love you.
Lala
ps don't forget your superpower.
@alannasaun
Originally from Kirkland, WA

EZRA MENAS
Originally from
Wichita, KS

Dear Ezra,

When the lights are bright again...I hope you remain steadfast in your dream to shift the structure of our existing Broadway, to one that centers Black Trans Liberation. I hope you continue to use your voice to build a more equitable, inclusive Broadway; one that actively creates opportunities for the Black community, the Indigenous community, the Latine community, the AAPI community, communities of color, 2SLGBTQQIA+ community, fat, neurodiverse, disabled, deaf and HOH communities and any other community directly disenfranchised by white supremacy.

I hope you remember that in order to imagine and create this Broadway, you must have hope, continue to listen, invest in collective care, and always follow the lead of the most marginalized person in the room. A better, stronger, truly inclusive Broadway is possible, and I hope you remain committed to the marathon of structural change with every single step.

With love,
Ezra
@Ezra_menas

Dear Nicholas,

When the lights are bright again you will have options and no longer need to conform to the rigorous demands of backstage existence. Life on a bus to get to a minimum 10 hour day/night career in a theatre with steep stairwells and meager ventilation was magical. But were you and your union brothers and sisters receiving fair wages in a country that claims to be the richest in the world? Thank God the union was able to extend benefits while the President lied about the virus that still has the world stage. **Strength comes from within.** You can't look to leadership for guidance. You really couldn't during that administration. You were out sick a week before Broadway went dark, and were willing to return with a lingering cough that was definitely Covid. Thankfully, your incredible boss and friend was able to cover your track with one swing that was available. This time has surfaced the dire needs of so many souls. You thought healthcare in the United States would be automatic during a pandemic....awe, cute. If the show doesn't open up before July you will be without insurance.

You first used your voice to reach out to your local union president with concerns about how to possibly return to work handling sweaty, potentially bloody costumes, as a face to face regular work practice in ultra tight changing nooks. We all need to rethink our workplace.

Was that Easter? Nobody got together. Maybe next year?

Oh...so calling unemployment for 3.5 hours daily for 4 weeks is useless. Here in America, I will just stop paying bills if that is what it means to be a part of the system. There are definitely more pressing issues to lose sleep over right now like if I'm dead from this cough, the bills will be fine!

Two hours registering for don't call them food stamps proves another waste of time.

In June your Broadway unemployed tenant realized it made no sense to keep that crash pad.

Oh yeah! Now we see why OSHA matters in a precious awareness class during July.

Your voice grew stronger when you dedicated hours phone banking Broadway for Biden. Drove that gloved hand to the mail-in ballot box under surveillance.

And thanks to Mom you empower with voiceover to open new doors.

> **And we will never be the same. WE will be better.**

Your voice has always been for the greater good. Now it has more focus. What kept you going was listening for the other voices that joined to move forward together. So much has unraveled like an exciting bolt of fabric. And we will never be the same. WE will be better.

Nicholas
Originally from Upper Saddle River, NJ

Dear PL2,

When the lights are bright again, I hope the light within you shines brighter than before and radiates and explodes out of your chest and eyes and fingertips and throat, blinding anyone who's ever said, "You can't."

I want you to continue to be a pillar of outspokenness, individualism, perseverance, compassion and unmitigated queer acceptance.

You are not dispensable.

You have a voice.

I want you to shine that light on sexual harassment, discrimination, predation, body-shaming and internalized homophobia.

I want there to be accountability for the way we talk to and treat one another, especially the marginalized.

You've shown strength when told, "You were the best singer we heard, but walking in the door you just screamed: homosexual" and fell to the NYC sidewalk in tears only to get up again. Strength when the essence of who you are was used as a weapon against you. An excuse.

Patience when a casting director stopped your song and said, "try and not sound like a cat being strangled" while your mother waited in Starbucks having flown in to be with you on your birthday.

Grace when an agent said you looked chubby and that you were, "not buff enough to be in the ensemble." Grace when a casting director repeatedly commented on your appearance, belittling and patronizing you saying, "I don't know where I would put you."

Boundaries when a former agent sent you unsolicited photos of their genitalia and you felt so violated.

Resilience when a creative team used your queerness as a

> **I want there to be accountability for the way we talk to and treat one another, especially the marginalized.**

punchline, because their own sexual struggles were apparent and your existence threatened their own insecurities.

Yet these moments were also met with a deafening silence for fear of retaliation or retribution.

I want the light within you to outshine all of this inspiring your vocal cords to scream, sing out and protest.

Stand your ground and never bow down.

While we're here, for this fleeting blip of time in the history of everything - I want to make this world better.

It all starts from within you.

You can do it.

And you can do it with love.

xoxoxo
PL2
@paullouislessard
Originally from Okemos, MI

> "I say we take the doors off the hinges entirely. We don't want them anymore."

ROB MCCLURE
Originally from
Philadelphia, PA

Dear Rob,

When the lights are bright again, you'll wonder how much of this time your 2-year-old daughter will remember. No longer able to spend every moment by her side, you will hope and pray that her little spirit retains these seasons spent loving each other so closely. You'll hope her future will be shaped, not just by the lessons we learned from Grover & Elmo in this time, but the ones we learned from Nick Cordero & Doreen Montalvo Mann & Rebecca Luker. The ones we learned from Stacey Abrams & Vanessa Warri. The ones we learned from John Lewis & Ruth Bader Ginsberg.

You'll be more in love with your wife than ever. She will have, once again, proven to you that when the shit hits the fan, you are strongest together.

You'll hope the family cuddle time was enough to counteract the screaming pundits in the background. You'll hope you didn't spend too much time on your phone. You'll hope you spoke out when you were needed and stepped back when you weren't.

After this mandatory time of reflection, you will have learned so much, but still know so little.

You'll sing again. You'll dance again. You'll tell stories again.

But—If theaters are churches, which I believe they are, then to what faith will you subscribe when the lights are bright again? Will you perpetuate an antiquated religion in favor of not upsetting the elders? Or will you insist that the doors swing wider than before?

Will you simply change the locks? Or remove them? I say we take the doors off the hinges entirely. We don't want them anymore. Some of the devout may have moments when they fear too many new congregants might push them out the back door. You must help them understand that a church built on a foundation of exclusion isn't one to be proud to attend.

Rob, when the lights are bright again…

Do not come back—come forward.

I'll be waiting,
Euphegenia Doubtfire
@mcclurerob

Dear Blake,

When the lights are bright again, be you. You fit the stereotypical goddamn mold of every colonizer who landed here centuries ago and when you walk into a room it's obvious. You're clearly a straight white guy from the Midwest.. Or South.. Or whatever the hell happens to your accent after 3 or 4 IPAs. Of course they're IPAs, you douchebag. But even though you look like every other suburban white kid who knows every word to Lil Wayne's No Ceilings mixtape, you have something unique to offer. You've watched intently as 2020 tore apart your entire way of living. You took in those $600 unemployment checks like fucking Grether's Pastilles during audition week. You're also overwhelmed with this sense of failure that you're not "using this time to your advantage." It makes you want to laugh, cry, yell, sleep, play with your dog, and yell. Did I say yell? I'd like to yell, please. I'm such a failure for having been given so much and squandering it.

What did you do about it? You tried writing that film about your mother's abusive family history. You outlined that play about your dad's incredibly southern family. You tried. But you thought (and still think), who the fuck cares? You know people do or would but in a world oversaturated with quirky white guys who have a slightly-yet-not-so-different opinion, you feel like you're Vanilla Ice and everyone else is Queen (both songs are bops, though). Isn't it time to let someone else to have the mic? Women are trying to overcome patriarchal oppression every time they walk down the street. Black men and women are still slaves to racial inequities set up by your ancestors. But aww… You don't have a purpose. A purpose is for the privileged. Everyone else is just living. So live!

You're always learning and unlearning and that process is important to have and important to share. When the lights are bright again, you have to meet that light with confidence and tell your specific story and celebrate stories unlike your own. Don't be afraid of being held accountable: **it's on white, straight men to hold themselves responsible for dismantling their ancestors' white supremacist institutions.** Now, go learn something other than "It All Fades Away."

With a side of ranch,
Blake
@blakewprice
Originally from Kentwood, MI

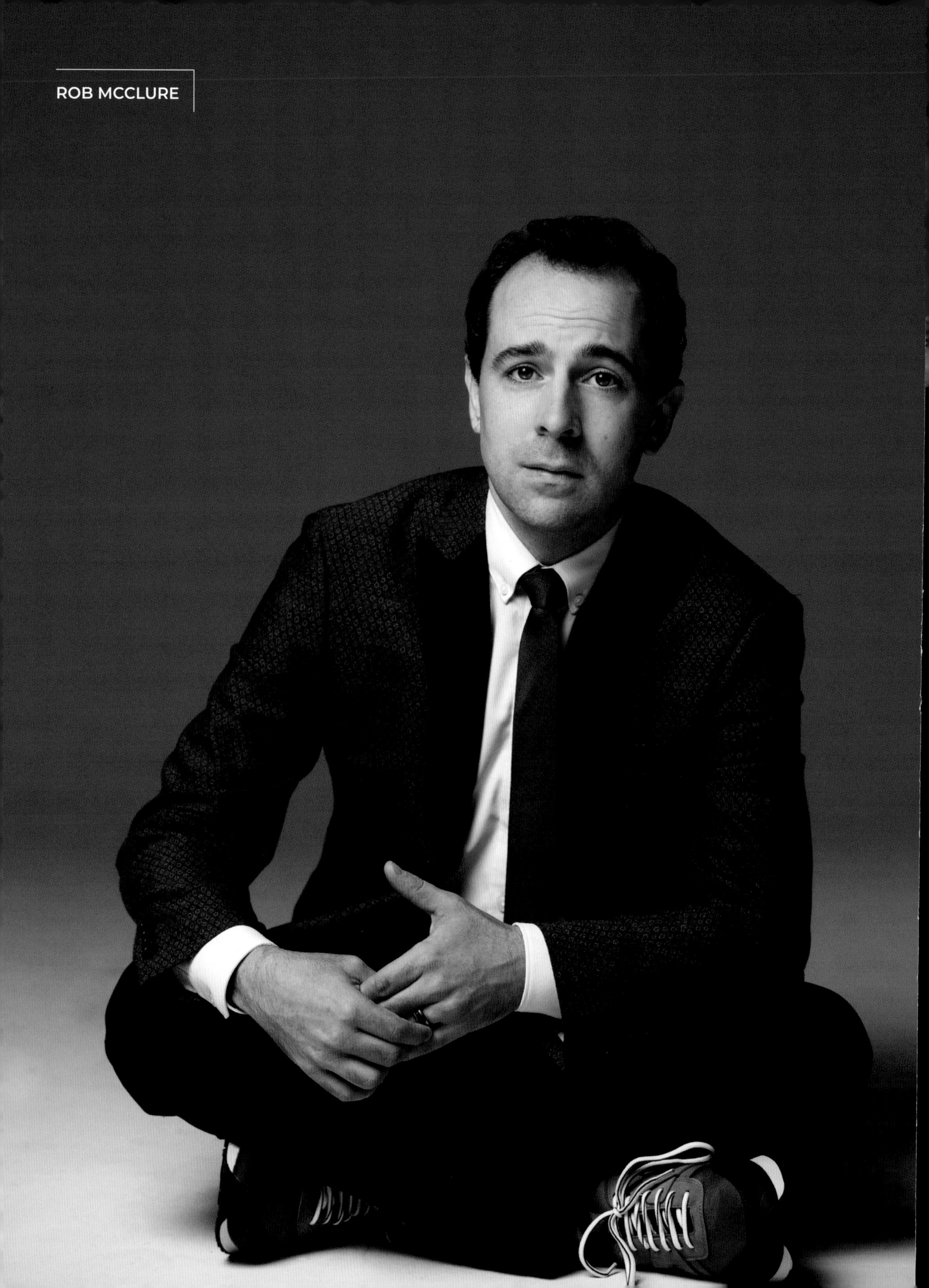

COURTNEY DANIELS
Hamilton Parish, Bermuda

NATTALYEE RANDALL
Springfield, IL

Dear Courtney and Nattalyee,

When the lights are bright again,

Remember that your worth is not based on the work you do or don't do on the stage. Instead, look at the honest human connections you've made while striving for a better place in this world. This year you took it to the streets for Black Lives and that is what matters the most. Who cares if you never perform on a stage again. At least you can walk away knowing that you fought hard for equality for Black, Indigenous, and people of color. You also fought for the trans, non binary, gender non conforming, Deaf, and disabled community.

You actually used your time during this pandemic to ignite change. Even if you didn't fully get the change you wanted, you got people to question their ethics and morals. You have brought awareness to mental health, self care, and knowing when not to engage in a capitalist machine. We are bigger than this business. We are human beings. Human beings with rights to inclusion. Human beings with rights to a safer work environment. Human beings with rights to fair pay. Be proud of yourself for creating that "good trouble."

You're by no means finished with this fight, but I do encourage you both to rest. Rest. Let your oppressors form into your allies and START THE WORK. No longer shall the oppressor sit comfortably with their supremacy. Rise up white man, rise up white woman. No longer will the marginalized community lift a finger to fix what you initially started. THEY must make room and hold space for those marginalized communities. THEY will sacrifice their privilege to elevate those who were born without it.

"Good Trouble" is what Nat and Court have displayed. Be proud my sistas. Be proud and pass the baton to those who are enriched with privilege.

Your rest awaits you.
BLACK POWER
@Nattalyee | @randomblackgirlllll

> ❝ We are human beings. Human beings with rights to inclusion. ❞

DAVON WILLIAMS
Originally from
Baltimore, MD

Dear Ally,

When the lights are bright again, always look to this letter when you are feeling flushed.

In less than a year, we recorded 26 episodes of the *The Receipts*, which provided over 2,300 hours of content regarding the American Theatre Industry. Riveting stuff… As of today, we have clocked over 118,750 views with a reach of over 750,000. This little internet show was able to garner the attention of Playbill, BroadwayWorld, Onstage Blog, Forbes, Deadline, The Daily Beast, The New York Times, Broadway News, NYS Music, Reddit, CBS Local News, and 60 Minutes with no marketing strategy, no public relations team, and no financial support.

We fell head first into topics such as electioneering, racial gaslighting, exploitation of Black outrage after the death of George Floyd, alleged embezzlement, workplace harassment, SAG-AFTRA's dispute with AEA, the flaws of the SET Agreement, safety protocols during COVID, bonding, drag in relation to theatre, town halls, bullying, the contributions of Black women, in-depth looks into navigating AEA leadership, creating an equitable space, contributions from the Negro Actors' Guild, audition systems, legal discrepancies, being an Arts Hero, caregiving, the exploration of labor law, and so many other pressing issues within the theatre industry. My inner nerd was satiated.

Through this show, over 500 people came together to develop the Black Theatre Matters Bill, and even more actively advocated for it. Thanks to the leaders of the #MarchOnBroadway, along with others such as ATB Talent, 3D Theatricals, Boxers (R.I.P.), Black Theatre Girl Magic, Native Son, Clubhouse influencers, Broadway Advocacy Coalition, Black Theatre Caucus, Bilingual Broadway, AFECT, Broadway for Racial Justice, the Broadway Hotdog, and the countless individuals who declared that their voice was enough to amplify this moment, the bill reached a majority before heading into the Actors' Equity Association's Inaugural Convention.

And, of course, none of this progress came without challenges. Though the Black Theatre Matters Bill passed at the convention, that same space was interrupted by a walkout due to racism. AEA, to this day, still refuses to acknowledge, in detail, the 3 day racist onslaught that its own BIPOC members of governance are begging for them to publicly address. To this day, AEA is actively protecting the names of the abusers who are still sitting in positions of power. The work of over 500 contributors was attacked with the weaponizing of a white woman's tears as our efforts were deemed "convoluted and irrelevant." The over 500 contributors were passively attacked a week beforehand by a seasoned AEA councilor who equated us to the likes of QAnon. Even though AEA agreed that the actions committed were

harmful, they still did nothing but give this aggressor a copy of the "code of conduct" policy. This same councilor, after insinuating that she was a victim in all of this, was later outed for casually using the "N" word numerous times in the presence of a Black castmate and his peers while on tour. To this day, he has not recovered, and she has still faced no repercussions. However, a BIPOC delegate is being put into a disciplinary hearing for reacting to her active gaslighting. Apparently, using the "N" word and reducing fellow union members to QAnon is not a problem for AEA, but having said councilor be told to "chill the [curse word] out" by a Latino identifying delegate in a meeting is enough license for her to actively pursue the "stripping" of his position. Does it surprise you that AEA complied with her request?

This councilor still actively sits in a position of power within AEA governance, with no outcry from the same AEA councilors who were the loudest "allies" and "civil rights leaders" during the past AEA election cycle, when race-baiting was a guaranteed path to winning. Where were these people during the convention, when I was forced to smile in a pink suit through a racist verbal assault? Understanding that if there was a reaction to what was happening to me, the entire Black Theatre Matters Bill would not have passed. It's been a month since that moment, and I still find myself mentally trapped in that space while my abuser continues to bask in an AEA protected life. Showing no accountability for her actions and no acknowledgment to the people she harmed, this same abuser has chosen the familiar tool of violence through silence. And even then, it has been made evident that she was just following orders from a political gang within AEA's governance, who fearfully hide in the shadows because they are wise enough to know that they should not be the face for the hate they give. At this convention, a Black man in a robe discussing economics was deemed violent by the standards of AEA. However, even in that racist space, a miracle happened, the Black Theatre Matters Bill passed.

If you walk away with anything, please let it be the fact

> **Where were these people during the convention, when I was forced to smile in a pink suit through a racist verbal assault?**

that this all happened in less than a year. Not because of some major following, campaign, or agenda, but because we dared to act… And yet, I still have one regret. When you came on to my team early in the development of the show, I had a tough time understanding you. When we first met, your abrasive way of communicating made it very tough to interact. I don't know what I did to win your trust, but I cherish the fact that you gave it. When you first told me what happened to you, I was still too ignorant to how things worked in this community. I foolishly believed that the public eye solved everything. I referenced the #MeToo Movement as if that moment in time ended all abuse in the world. I kept your secret because, just like Oprah describes her dream interview with O.J. Simpson, I would actively fantasize about us doing the episode where you would name your abuser for all to hear. I imagined AEA's council calling an emergency meeting, removing that councilor, and all of us uniting behind you. That's the thing about hope; it makes way for the greatest of miracles, but it blinds us to the hard truths of life. Reality showed up when I met a woman who came forward with eight other survivors in the New York Times. With such a major platform, nothing happened. Tears ran hearing her story. That same abuser went on to live a full life until they passed away during the pandemic. That name that had brought so many harm went on to be exhumed in a moment of reverence among the leaders of our union.

You told me that you had found peace before we went on this journey. Dealing with my own traumas, I got lost in the idea that peace meant direct resolve. No justice, no peace, right? If your abuser wasn't brought to some form of perceived justice, then what was the point? We have accomplished so much, but at the cost of your peace… And for that, I apologize. The biggest lesson I have learned through this endeavor, is that this is not a safe space. When the lights are bright again, please remember that taking center is optional.

Davon Williams
@daywilling

CREATIVITY

Dear Grace,

When the lights are bright again… I hope you remember your resilience. I hope you remember everything from the last 365+ days. As a trauma response we often choose to make new memories in place of the bad ones. This is a story to future me–the girl who may have forgotten her strength.

A girl was performing her solo show for a very humble audience in the Lower East Side as people started to stay home at the beginning of March 2020.

As soon as the quarantine notice hit, everyone in the apartment abandoned her, the beautiful living room, and an adorable cat. Fortunately, it was filled with magnificent sunshine and she began painting again for the first time in years. Suddenly DMs with a friend turned into short voice memos, which turned into FaceTimes, which turned into 9-hour engagements.

As the days passed, she began recording her stories, watching more movies, and using watercolors to paint her thoughts. In an attempt to get out of the months and months of solitude, she and the friend safely road tripped from NY to GA. At the first public restroom stop, she tried to act very cool while she was absolutely terrified the entire time. Something about taking a journey during the end of the world with someone who had only almost exclusively existed on a phone screen created such an exciting and challenging dynamic. They'd not really been in each other's spaces and had to learn how to "people" again.

When she returned to my gorgeous sun-filled home, it felt sad and stale. Shortly thereafter, following an escalating abusive encounter, her mental health plummeted and she was admitted to a facility. Upon release, the girl was strongly advised to not return to the toxic domicile. She had to evacuate her former sanctuary within hours with the help of a small tribe of women, to whom she owes everything. Since then, she has been a nomad, still writing and painting wherever there is a flat surface.

> **I hope you remember your resilience.**

My friends are so much more now, the cat is well, and she learned that home is where she feels safe and loved–it's within her.

The first thing I'm doing coming out of the pandemic is a weekend of performances of the same solo show I was workshopping in 2020. I actually cannot imagine the feeling that will overcome my body stepping into the light again. So much of my life has fallen apart and been rebuilt, I know the audience shares the same experiences, perhaps the stories will bind us.

When the lights are bright again, she'll outshine them, she'll be strong, and best of all, she'll realize she's home.

Grace
@itsgraceaki
Originally from Dalton, GA

> **At the same time, you will have unearthed a dormant spark inside yourself to, literally, write your own songs and live out a personal rock dream.**

> ## You will rediscover and continue growing your imagination, your sense of exploration, your artistic self.

Dear Jenny,

When the lights are bright again, you will have a front row seat to watch this first illumination. You will bear witness to this alchemy, this stage magic, before all other patrons. You will catch this light in the eyes of every Broadway professional as they reignite their passionate crafts, building to a perfect collaboration with throngs of equally ardent colleagues and friends.

When the lights are bright again, you will see different hues, hear different stories, feel new experiences never fully realized on stage. For their time is long overdue. These songs and soliloquies need to be celebrated and shared to re-circuit the single-wire filaments that have lit these stages for far too long.

When the lights are bright again, you will look back on days, months, years of time that you spent working daily, diligently, to bring these lights back on. **Pivot, step; pivot, step.** At the same time, you will have unearthed a dormant spark inside yourself to, literally, write your own songs and live out a personal rock dream.

Now get back to work! There are press releases to write, photo calls to supervise, interviews to schedule and tickets to sell so others can watch these bright lights shine, again.

Jenny
@jenepiphany
Originally from San Diego, CA

Dear E,

When the lights are bright again, you will embrace your artistry with grace and forgiveness. Just because you took an office job during the pandemic does not make you less of an artist. Even on days you don't feel creative, **YOU ARE A CREATIVE.** In this time of darkness, you have not lost those pieces of yourself despite not always sensing them at the surface. You will rediscover and continue growing your imagination, your sense of exploration, your artistic self. Don't forget it is not a race; when the lights are bright again, they are not shining upon a play button that has been pressed on a competition that was formerly paused. You can look at those bright lights and be reminded of why you love them in the first place, and get ready to revel in the stories to be told. No pressure, just enjoy the magic of music, art, dance, and storytelling. Break a leg. :)

Love,
Elana
@elanavalastro
Originally from South Burlington, VT

Dear Garrett,

When the lights are bright again you'll feel at home. You'll remember where you belong and the purpose of all your hard work and patience. Soon, you will be surrounded by the community that sees you and loves you. **You have so much to offer and more light and music to give.** Until that time, remember to focus on your daily tasks, practice gratitude, and continue striving for truth and beauty in your creative and personal endeavors.

Be bold,
Garrett
@the_garrett_taylor_show
Originally from New York, NY

SERGIO TRUJILLO
Originally from
Colombia via
Toronto, Canada

Dear Sergio,

When the lights are bright again, you will gaze over the precipice of this pandemic, and you will dance. You will dance for those we lost. You will dance for the budding youthful talent not yet seen. You will dance for sorrow and pleasure, doubt and joy. You will look through the tunnel of the last year and celebrate all the great accomplishments you have somehow managed to achieve. You will find optimism and a sense of peace, even through your helplessness. You will remember how your emotions shifted as often as news stories on social media. Above all, you will feel fortunate for the quality time spent with your husband and son, as all sense of urgency and distractions faded away.

When the lights are bright again, you will not regret a single day you spent supporting your husband as he worked long days raising funds for artists. You will continue to see how essential your partnership is to your artistic life, and how it brings humanity into your work. You will recall how young dancers you spoke with throughout this crisis made you feel bright and alive each day. You will always be inspired by their passion and determination to turn their hopelessness into hope.

When the lights are bright again, "you" will become "we" once more. Not only the "we" of virtual meetings, but the "we" of an ensemble gathering in studios and theaters. You will move forward with friendships and relationships with colleagues, somehow made stronger through mutual struggle. **Now more than ever, you will create opportunities for Latinx artists like yourself.**

The lights will be bright once more. You will succeed in the endeavors developed during the time of Covid, and you will be a vessel for change in this industry. You will prop up those in the shadows, who have waited too long for their turn to take the floor. And yes, you will dance. But not alone. Never alone.

In Motion,
Sergio
@sergiotrujillo1

"You will dance for sorrow and pleasure, doubt and joy."

Dear Jonathan,

When the lights are bright again…. You know what they say… "it's always darkest just before they turn on the lights." My question is, "what will you discover when they turn on those lights?"

If only I had Professor Marvel's crystal ball and I was Dorothy asking, "what do you see?"

I know you are 60 years old and you have accomplished so much in the creative arts field that I can tell you it was not for naught… I know you will be able to be happy again, I know you will be able to breathe again, sleep with the unabashed joy and anticipation of waking up to go to rehearsal, I know you will be able to be in the room where it happens and of a community, a community I know you love so much.

That is if you want it and will undertake what is there for you.

I know the isolation is what is depressing you, being separated from that community I am sure is intolerable. I can only tell you that it will get better, it will. I know you know that, and this challenge is just that, A CHALLENGE. **Humanity and civilization are being challenged** and you must be stronger than, be bigger than, rise above the fray and be the good creative soul you are. Your creativity won't go away – you can't make it; it will always bite you and tell you how incredibly hungry it is. It won't stop until it gets its fill and it never will…

Your creativity is who you are and when the lights are bright again you will be able to see that, and having learned what you learned from this period of pause and isolation, frustration and fear, you will be a better person.

I can tell you if you look deeply into Professor Marvel's crystal ball, artists will be in demand and the riches you will have because of this is yet unknown, and will be so very powerful.

So, I tell you to be patient, for you will shine brighter when the lights are bright again.

With Love Now and Forever,
Jonathan
@jcstuart2
Originally from New York, NY

> "Your creativity won't go away – you can't make it; it will always bite you and tell you how incredibly hungry it is. It won't stop until it gets its fill and it never will…"

Dear Amanda,

When the lights are bright again…you'll go back to work in the industry. You're getting a world premiere production of one of your plays (to whoever is reading this, come see the show)! Your potential remains untapped, and the opportunities are still limitless.

A question lingers in your mind, however, and you don't mean to be cliché and reference Hamilton: Will I ever be satisfied?

During the Broadway shutdown, you were not being complacent…you've made strides by singing in virtual concerts and joining the Dramatists Guild, for example. You've also written several lyrics- which is nothing new- but one song relates directly to that question you've been rolling around.

"I've had dreams my whole life

That didn't rely on anyone.

But now I'm on the edge of a knife,

And I don't know where to run.

If I had everything at my beck and call,

Would it mean anything at all?

The world is not enough."

When the lights are bright again, you'll have to confront your neverending sense of ambition and longing even more. "There's more to see than can ever be seen." That's from The Lion King. Good luck.

Yours,
Amanda
@marqueegirlstagram
Originally from Staten Island, NY

Dear Sara,

When the lights are bright again you will instantly remember who you are. Or should I say, who you were, but now with a new and improved pair of eyes. I am so proud of you for the hardships you have overcome while the lights have been out. The amount of growing you've done has been immeasurable, and incredibly important. I hate that it took the lights going out to allow the time and space for that, but you've always been a true believer of the universe calling attention to things when it is most needed. The pace at which you run your life rarely allows for slowing down and taking a step back, but I think we can all agree how important it is to do sometimes.

As easy as it is to focus on the negative events of this time—and you have endured an abnormal amount—you have been able to turn your pain into strength. To dig deep into who you really are, and what you really want out of life. The answers were supported by the same dream each and every time - You want to create art. We have now seen a world and life without art, and you've found that to dim your internal light as well. But Sara, you are doing exactly what you were born to do. Waiting for the lights to come back on has never not been an option. You have so many things to do, Sara! For you, and for those who are no longer with us. **Be patient, take deep breaths, and please be kind to yourself.** We will get there, and when we do, you will hold your people and your community closer than ever - literally you won't be able to stop hugging everyone so BE WARNED. It will be the most incredible feeling. PLEASE hold on to the lessons you've learned during this time. There is still a lot of work to do personally and as a community going forward, and the things you've gained will be essential in propelling you in the right direction. You should also know that you have the most incredible family and friends in the world. They are the sole reason you've made it this far. When you need someone to lean on, just know that they would never in a million years let you give up your passion just because of a temporary power outage.

Hold on, strong one. Almost there. Love always,
Sara
@estygrl
Originally from Gorham, ME

CLINT RAMOS
Originally from
Cebu, Philippines

Dear Clint,

When the lights are bright again, brace yourself and wrap everyone with your love for the theatre.

Let your desire to make it better be understood as a fierce expression of that love.

Let that expression be the clarity with which you move and let empathy, justice and action be the fuel for your art.

Create what you love most only with passion, resolve and service.

And, as you walk home, every night, after a long day's work – I wish you peace and long, deep breaths.

With love,
Clint
@clintramos

"...brace yourself and wrap everyone with your love for the theatre."

Dear Jay,

When the lights are bright again, it'll be as magical as the first time. Maybe even more so.

Since you were a kid, theater has been your chosen home; your sanctuary; your escape; at times, your drug. This year, you've had to sit with yourself in discomfort and unease about the future of the institution that helped define you. You've had to reckon with your community's, your industry's, and your own shortcomings when it comes to social justice.

The reckoning continues.

This year, even without theater, you have been able to support yourself and continue creating in this vulnerable time. You've often thought it was your right to be able to do so; you now understand it's your privilege. While I'm proud of how you have pivoted, innovated, educated, and stayed active as an artist in this time, there's nothing quite as sweet as intimate collaboration with your fellow man. They say that you don't know what you've got 'til it's gone, and you've never felt that more than this year.

Remember that moment of collective darkness in a theater awaiting your entrance, or nervous anticipation of your peers making theirs? Remember how the air felt electric, and the butterflies swarmed in your stomach? That's all this year has been - a collective, prolonged darkness of nerves and anticipation. Hang on. We're almost there. The magic you have cherished all these years will be alive and well when the lights are bright again.

Take what you've learned, and let's keep on keeping.

Measure In Love,
Jay
@Jay_A_Johnson
Originally from Fort Worth, TX

Dear Lauren,

When the lights are bright again, I will soak up the sights, sounds, smells, and feelings of a theatre waiting in anticipation for the show to start.

Having said goodbye to onstage work in 2018 when I left the National Tour of *Wicked*, I was in the middle of a masters in March 2020. I had also just choreographed my first professional production and was elated to have been chosen for an observership alongside Graciela Daniele which was supposed to begin in April 2020. This would have been the highlight and finale of my two years pursuing my MFA in Musical Theatre: the opportunity to work with one of the greatest female legends in musical theatre history. That opportunity was canceled.

Among all of the disappointments, I have to give supreme thanks to my students who have been a big reason I have made it through. The best thing that came out of 2020 is that I started an Assistant Professor position at Indiana University. When so many were stuck dancing on Zoom at home, the university let me teach limited masked students in person in a real dance studio. **I have watched them all persevere through this crazy and uncertain time.** They are continuing to pursue a BFA in Musical Theatre when the future of Broadway, Tours, and Regional Theatres is in question. Their drive and hunger to pursue it lives on. Therefore, theatre doesn't need to return for me or my generation for that matter (although I know the world would crumble without it). Theatre needs to return so my students get their moment onstage, under lights, with real people in seats watching them, followed by real human reaction, in real time.

Now that I am a full-time professor, director, and choreographer I can't wait to be one of those audience members in the seats cheering on my students. They are the ones who trained daily singing and dancing in masks for over a year. They deserve to be seen and appreciated for their will, commitment, and belief that theatre will survive this.

5678,
Lauren
@laurenhaughton
Originally from Atlanta, GA

Dear Analise,

When the lights are bright again... never forget who you are.

It's been a year. I don't really know how I'm feeling. I'm sad and sometimes I blame everyone that my first ounce of an independent life was ripped from me right after it started, yet at the same time I'm super grateful that I had time to breathe and focus on other things.

I'm really proud of you. You were living the life you had always wanted. Your first apartment. Your first principal role on Broadway. Your first show as an adult. And three days into your first week of this life, you were put right back where you were before. You try to put on a brave face and push through all obstacles that come your way, but I know this was a hard pill to swallow. The first few months were an endless rotation of the same routine and you were still convinced that *Doubtfire* would be back shortly.

You slowly found a way to get yourself out of that bubble of sadness. The second you picked up your guitar you never looked back. **Writing saved you and I want you to take my advice and never stop.**

Would you have known one year ago that you are coming out with an EP this year?

Did you ever think you'd be back in college and have three more classes left until you graduate?

Did you know how much you'd cherish this time with your family?

I'm really proud of how you handled this. It was an awful thing that happened, but look at all of the things you were able to accomplish!

When the lights are bright again, never forget who you are. Never forget sitting in your room writing and reading and learning new things. Never forget the good times and the times when you wanted to wake up from this scary dream. They have helped you grow as a human and as an artist. I can't wait to watch your new human self up on that stage again. Keep your head up.

Analise
@analise.scarpaci
Originally from Staten Island, NY

> "Never forget the good times and the times when you wanted to wake up from this scary dream."

Dear Jimmy,

When the lights are bright again, I hope you never take for granted how lucky you are to be in a space full of people sharing the gift of live theatre. More importantly, I hope you never again resort to waiting around or begging others for the opportunity to create art.

You love musical theatre with your whole heart, but over the past few years you've been struggling to figure out your role in the industry. You find yourself questioning why you lack the motivation to go to dance class, to take a voice lesson or brush up on your acting skills; sadly, it took a worldwide theatre shutdown for you to realize why.

As a child, it was drilled into your head that once you book a Broadway show, you'll have "made it." So you trained tirelessly in hopes of reaching that final goal; but with all of the focus on that commercial success, you started to lose your joy for the art itself. Then suddenly, the entire industry shuts down and every theatre artist finds themselves jobless. **The hierarchy is destroyed and there's no longer an elite group of people on Broadway.** You feel a weight lifted off your shoulders because the pressure you constantly feel to try and get ahead is gone. You start to see performers turning to virtual theatre; but there's no equity and non-equity online, there's no Broadway of YouTube, and money is no longer a factor. The toxicity of the industry has been removed and the entire theatre community has come together in a way I've never seen before. We all take a step back and look at the stories we have been telling and who has been lucky enough to tell them. We look at the flaws within our industry and start to have conversations about the changes that need to be made once theatre returns.

The art form that you feel so passionately about has been taken away entirely, yet you feel more inspired than you've felt in years. There are no longer gatekeepers, and for the first time in your life you aren't begging anyone for the opportunity to make art. **You start to fearlessly create again, and suddenly you have more faith in your gifts than ever before.**

So when the lights are bright again, make sure you hold onto that faith. Continue to share the immense amount of love you have for this art form in any way possible- you don't need anyone's permission. Lead with love, and advocate for the stories and artists that you believe in most. Always remember to do what makes you most happy and believe unconditionally. You are special.

Love,
Jimmy
@jimmylarkin | @letshearitforthechoice
Originally from Natick, MA

> "The art form that you feel so passionately about has been taken away entirely, yet you feel more inspired than you've felt in years. There are no longer gatekeepers, and for the first time in your life you aren't begging anyone for the opportunity to make art."

Dear Robert,

ROBERT HARTWELL
Originally from
Raleigh, NC

When the lights are bright again, your life will look different. You had no idea watching Ephraim and Derrick's final performance in *Ain't Too Proud* in February 2020 that it would be the final Broadway show you'd see for 18 months. You had no idea you would lose two aunts to a virus that would disproportionately affect people that looked just like you.

You fought to choose joy. Some days have been harder than others, but you've leaned on love. You've leaned on the hope that your best days are still ahead of you. You've learned that you can always speak a better word. You've learned the power of pivoting. And most importantly, you've learned that you are human, and therefore deserving of rest.

Nothing about this time has been easy, but I know that you will look back and be proud that you kept going. You will emerge from this experience with a sense of mindfulness, and with even more awareness of the support and love that surrounds you. You will fully embrace the people that believe in your heart and trust in the impact you are trying to have on this world.

However, as you move back into the world, I want you most of all to lean into ownership. You love to create that opportunity for others, and it's okay for you to manifest and take part in that abundance as well. The windows of opportunity ahead of you will not harm you. You will always be kept.

Never forget that you can do hard things. Trust that there is more good for you than darkness against you. Lean into the remembrance that in this dark period, there was still immense light and goodness fighting for you. Your still being here is proof that the best is yet to come – and that is something that can never be taken away.

It will all come together even better than you can imagine. You just need to let it.

And finally, when you step back into the studio, on the stage, or into your new home, know that Aunt Paulette and Aunt Mildred are saying "that's *awesome*, Rob".

Robert
@sirroberttakespics

> " You fought to choose joy. Some days have been harder than others, but you've leaned on love. "

"Never forget that you can do hard things. Trust that there is more good for you than darkness against you."

> *Volunteering throughout the election, volunteering at the Soup Kitchen, and looking after elderly performing artists.*

Dear Grant,

When the lights are bright again you are going to Love that moment of anticipation before the lights come up or the curtain rises beyond what you ever have before. This will be true, whether you are in the house or standing at places, backstage. In addition, your next dreaded Tech Rehearsal is going to feel like a Hoe-Down!

I have to pat you on the back, my friend. You have been kicking ass this pandemic! Volunteering throughout the election, volunteering at the Soup Kitchen, and looking after elderly performing artists. All that and still managing to safely present In-Person theater by commissioning and producing The Park Bench Plays, you should be proud! After all, the brightest stage light ever known is the sun! It makes you feel embarrassed for our large institutions that most failed to present anything in-person throughout the warm months of 2020.

Your anger at your union's ineptitude and hampering stance will subside over time. You just have to focus on all the wonderful people who have shown up with spirit for your efforts, and asked you to participate in their big-hearted endeavors.

I look forward to kicking my Zoom account to the curb for a while, and being in a room with a beautifully diverse group of people freely tossing ideas around, when the lights are bright again!

With joy and respect,
Grant Neale
@nomadtheatrical
Originally from New Baltimore, MI

Dear Brown Tigress,

When the lights are bright again, you will be glowing. Although you're not sure when, you can still dream and hope and pray.

Who knew that plans for the church Women's Convention or the Sunday School Easter Program would never come to fruition? Building the set for the crucifixion scene, fitting the soldiers for their costumes, fussing over who gets to wear the enormous angel wings, and the liturgical dances.

You were mad, hurt, disappointed, confused, worried, and scared. Remember when you realized you were slipping into a mental state that would take you to the point of no return? But you prayed and eventually climbed up out of that dark place—Yea. You have written over 30 plays, and a month before Covid-19, you realized you wanted so much more than just participating in festivals. Your love for Shen Yun and Sight and Sound Theater encouraged you to stay hopeful that your dreams are only a bright light away from dawning.

Eventbrite became your best hang out spot with many webinars such as Building Blocks for Starting a Business. So, in a weird sense, Covid-19 helped you. Your websites are up, you have registered your business name, formed your LLC, and completed a great business plan through the help of your SCORE mentor.

So, Brown Tigress, listen, I know some days you still tell yourself that time is slipping away, and at your age, this is a far-off dream. **But on your crying days, keep writing**. When you feel like you're wasting your time, keep writing because when the lights are bright again, you will be standing at the door of your local theater with your name "creativeworshipINK" written in bold letters. Yes, you got this girl, so keep on doing you until the lights are bright again.

Stay blessed, stay strong, stay safe, stay hopeful.
Brown Tigress
@creativeworshipink
Originally from Howard Beach, NY

> Remember that survival is of the flesh and creating is of the soul. You have survived for a long time. For way too long. And I know that has broken your own heart. I also know that you have tried and that you're tired, but I still know that you always have the strength to try... one more time.

Dear José Leonardo,

When the lights are bright again...

stop surviving and choose to **create** instead. Find a way to create full-time. Give yourself a chance and go after those opportunities. Remember that survival is of the flesh and creating is of the soul. You have survived for a long time. For way too long. And I know that has broken your own heart. I also know that you have tried and that you're tired, but I still know that you always have the strength to try... one more time. I've seen you do it, all these years. Your soul needs you. I need you.

When the lights are bright again...

keep risking being **vulnerable** in all your works. When you show yourself vulnerable, there is a great possibility that somebody else will recognize themselves in that vulnerability, and when two or more people recognize themselves in their own vulnerability the world becomes softer.

When the lights are bright again...

don't forget **who you are**. All these years of stumbling and learning have taught you how to fall, and each fall has freed you of something about yourself that you didn't need. And it's that same ongoing process of healing that has shaped you into who you are today. And who you are is enough. If your heart fell and broke so many times it was because it needed to be open. So, don't be afraid to keep it that way, it's who you are, it's the only way your true self and your art can shine.

So, when the lights are bright again...

...will you finally go after all of our **dreams**? I hope so. Don't lose faith now. You are here. Exactly where you should be. With the gift of a new beginning and endless opportunities ahead. Don't be afraid of the storm. It's better to dance in it. I will always be taking you by the hand.

Your little dreamer,
José Leonardo
@esjoseleo
Originally from Morovis, Puerto Rico

CONNECTION

Dear Taylor,

When the lights are bright again, remember the light inside you has always been aflame. Perhaps, it has dimmed or burned so intensely that it left you overwhelmed, unable to express your sadness–but that light never left you.

At the beginning of 2020, you were the Associate Choreographer of *Fly* at La Jolla Playhouse. You were exhausted and exhilarated simultaneously. You were nervous and confident simultaneously. Your light was forever burning of the love you possess for this art.

Because of COVID, it may seem like you haven't had the time or space to process this experience–what felt like the beginning of something wonderful. But guess what.. you have.

While quarantining in Massachusetts with your family, your light led you to what keeps your spirit bright. Helping your mom adjust to virtual teaching required patience and communication representative of those 10 out of 12 tech rehearsals just months before. Planning your parents' 30th at-home anniversary with your brother brought back the fun of creating an experience for a specific audience. Sitting in the driveway with your dad discussing the intricacies of the civil unrest in our country further extends the importance of shedding light on the larger themes of our world in our art.

Even when it felt like you were running on fumes, there was something there to add fuel to that fire. It was your desire for creativity and connection.

When the physical lights of theater are bright again, bring your best pair of sunglasses, because our collective light is going to be so bright.

Holding onto hope,
Taylor McMahon
@taylorjmcmahon
Originally from Astoria, NY

Dear Matt,

When the lights are bright again, you will appreciate how much this art form connects you with other people. You will not take for granted the ability to sit in a dark room and feel things with a bunch of strangers. You will appreciate the **EXPERIENCE** of live theater–the pre-show dinner, the post-show drinks, all of it. And you will value the impact that our work has on everyone–helping people to connect. You will relish the anticipation of half hour, the backstage silliness, the first downbeat, the adrenaline rush of leaving a vamp at precisely the right time, the bleary late night production meetings after tech... Also, this pause taught you even more about how much you love teaching. I hope you won't forget that.

Stay in it. You love it all.
Matt
@mstern303
Originally from Boston, MA

> ...you will value the impact that our work has on everyone–helping people to connect.

Dear whoever you may be,

> ...your community of actors...you will continue to uplift every single one of them as you all face a **NEW Broadway**...

Dear Keala,

When the lights are bright again...what will be the first thing you do? You know the first people you will contact will be every stage door "Richie" & "Freddie" & "Sunny" that you have ever known and rejoice. Then you will most likely blow up the cell phones of every single stagehand "Manny" & "Petey" & "Fran" & "Del" & "Keister" & "Brettski" you have ever known and raise a glass to them virtually. And, last but not least, your community of actors...you will continue to uplift every single one of them as you all face a **NEW Broadway**; one that breaks all unspoken rules from days gone by, revealing an unchartered path of unbounded expressive freedom, ready for the taking. The fire within has been fed. Your time is now. Buckle up! LET'S DO THIS!!!!!!

Love Yourself Always,
Keala
@realkealasettle
Originally from Laie, HI

When the lights are bright again, that moment of distancing yourself in a theater house full of peers while the director tells you theater is going on a hiatus until further notice will seem like a bad dream.

That absolute breakdown you had in your car, as your face flooded and your heart struggled to breathe in your stomach, will be merely a testament to what this business means to you.

Those mistrials of attempting to convey honesty and eagerness through a laptop screen and sending away your dreams via email will be tragically poetic once the lights are bright again.

And don't you dare forget that awful and awkward call back you had on a Discord server where you felt so out of place and alone.

One good thing though, is that through all of this **you were never alone**. Theater-folk all across the planet also imagined walking to a rehearsal every time they stepped onto a sidewalk. They also stared at their ceilings until 4 am while darkness encroached their vision. They also melted onto a bathroom floor just to feel the cool tile and cry until they were numb.

This time was unfair to creatives, to theater-folk, and to you.

But when the lights are bright again, your yearning will be quenched, and you will drown so deeply in their pools that it will feel like the first time you ever took a breath.

Returning, will feel as if you just stepped out of a kayak that's been jutting in the ocean and your family has rushed to envelop you.

In a way, you will feel like the Grinch or Tin Man, just receiving a heart and aching at the backflips it is performing behind your ribs.

And it will be just as sweet as your first bite of a Schmackary's snickerdoodle cookie while you sit on a rooftop watching the sunrise over NYC for the first time.

When the lights are bright again?
You will be home.
Whoever you may be
@brianna_west
Originally from Billings, MT

> I hope becoming a mother deepens your artistry.

ELIZABETH STANLEY
Originally from
Camp Point, IL

Dear Elizabeth,

When the lights are bright again, I hope you will really, really take in the preciousness of every live audience. I hope you will be able to hug your castmates and hold them tightly–and that you do it often. I hope you buy stock in waterproof mascara (you're going to need it!). I hope that watching and performing in live theatre can once again give you a vessel to process your deepest unnameable feelings. I hope that singing and sharing and breathing the same air as those around you feels as **sacred** as it did when you first fell in love with the experience. I hope you recognize all the magic around you. I hope you find an **exhale** from all that has burdened you for the past year and half, and I hope that the audience does too.

I hope that all the grief and loss and sadness of this current time deepen your empathy and make you a better listener. I hope whatever amount of pain we have all felt in our own different ways, each of us now can feel a joy that surpasses that! I hope we all feel reborn, renewed, alive again, a deeper, fuller, richer version of our truest selves.

And speaking of being born–I hope that you feel supported as a working mother. I hope you say "yes" to help, and say "no" to being superwoman. I hope becoming a mother deepens your artistry. I hope you are able to bring your baby backstage and I hope they know their extended family–all the aunties and uncles of the theatre! I hope their tiny but fully-formed heart can feel what a blessing it is to be surrounded by such a creative and welcoming community.

I hope the **harmony** you've so missed creating with other voices is a theme which vibrates beyond singing, beyond the stage, and beyond your work in the theatre. I hope creating harmony with others in as many ways as possible is a global goal, a lesson we have learned, a value we all feel called to uphold.

Until then…keep going. Keep the faith.

I love you,
Elizabeth
@el.stans

Dear Mary-Mitchell,

When the lights are bright again, you will not take anything for granted.

You will appreciate the magic of theater. The sound of an audience getting quiet at the top of a show will be the best sound in the world.

Art connects us.

Connection is everything.

When the lights are bright again, we will bring that connection to the world and begin to heal.

Holding onto hope,
Mary-Mitchell
@MaryMitchellc
Originally from New York, NY

Dear Joy,

When the lights are bright again... bask in the glow of togetherness of all forms. But remember what you found in the loneliness.

You were more honest in the silence.

Remember your privilege. Embrace the gray area between happiness and grief. Savor the mundane.

Holding onto hope,
Joy
@joydclark
Originally from Stockton, CA

Dear Jason,

When the lights are bright again, you will be there. You hear me? **You're gonna be there.**

Love,
Jason
@jasonwise
Originally from New York, NY

Dear Aaron,

When the lights are bright again there's one particular item I'm excited to see. **Cake**. No seriously! Think of all the cake we've missed out on enjoying. It's common backstage to celebrate birthdays. You buy the cake for the next birthday celebrant, and so on. You could walk through the stage door having a bad day and see that cake box sitting in the stairwell and POOF – your day just got better.

That leads me to backstage snacks in general. Just about every night at the theater, there's some sort of new snack – cupcakes from a new bakery trying to drum up business, a crudité platter leftover from a between-show baby shower, burnt cookies from someone who couldn't bear to toss the batch or unwanted tortilla chips from someone's Chipotle order.

"Did you see wardrobe is hosting a pancake brunch?!" "Stage Management has the new chips from Trader Joe's!" "The crew is having a BBQ taste test." "Where'd you go for dinner after the matinee?" These are sounds that fly through a theater faster than Patti LuPone's high belt.

I miss all of that…but let's be real. At the root of it, it's not the food I miss. I miss the interactions, camaraderie and shared joy that springs from these culinary happenings. I miss gathering in a crowded stairwell while singing "Happy Birthday." I miss staying late in the dressing room after the show for a shared glass of wine. I miss signing posters for BC/EFA while trying not to get pizza stains on them. I miss sharing these experiences with my friends and colleagues and I can't wait for us all to be together again. And when that time comes, if anyone wants to bring me a slice of Amy's Bread Black & White cake, I won't complain.

Love ya,
Aaron
@aaronkab
Originally from Carlinville, IL

Dear Loobs,

When the lights are bright again, you will see the theatre community beside you standing, all of you looking up at your favorite marquee, with tears falling as your faces are smiling. As you await to enter your favorite theatre, the world will stand still, as everyone takes in the moment: this is the void we always wanted to fill. We will finally see each other again after so long! We have come back home! You and the theatre missed each other. During this intermission, thank you for keeping the heart of the theatre community beating by posting covers of songs from different musicals you were singing; by always sharing news about what's happening in the theatre world we're craving; and by simply sending messages of support to your favorite artists whose jobs were temporarily cut short. At the end of this pandemic, you can take a bow, knowing that you did your part, then and now, in making sure that the theatre community would survive, eventually getting back up, stronger and ready to thrive. But when you finally get to your new normal, keep the biggest lesson you learned from staying home immortal: **you are never alone in your struggles**; just reach out and someone will pull you out from dark tunnels. Keep your passion for the theatre burning! You will get more of it as you share them with others who are also yearning. This, our love for theatre proves.

As always,
Loobs.
@Patrickloobs
Originally from Manila

> As you await to enter your favorite theatre, the world will stand still, as everyone takes in the moment: this is the void we always wanted to fill.

> **"**And I feel an excited wave of emotion come through my body as I think about waiting off stage in the dark to enter for the first time.**"**

Dear Sarah,

When the lights are bright again there will be joy! Artists are a part of something very special that is hard to explain, almost like a secret club, with no admission fee. Anyone can join this club, what's required is the deep rooted passion for telling story and wanting to share with people all over the world. This has been a time of reflection to appreciate the gifts I have been given. I am able to express myself through song and dance, and that is something not everyone can say. I long for the moment that the show I was in, *Mean Girls*, starts up and running again. And I feel an excited wave of emotion come through my body as I think about waiting off stage in the dark to enter for the first time. Looking onto the stage from the wings has been a cathartic experience since I was a kid and knew that theatre is what I was meant to do. When those stage lights are bright again it will be a symbol of hope that artists are resilient and strong and can handle anything that comes at them. There was no playbook for all of us to grieve together, but being a part of a community that understands that art is important is unbelievable. I know that my fellow artists and colleagues are up for the challenge and will, with humility pick right back up where we left off, just a little bit older and wiser (and my costumes a little bit tighter).

Looking forward to what the future holds,
Sarah
@saritacrane
Originally from Miami, FL

Dear Sally and Wyman,

When the lights are bright again you will see more people in costumes than in masks. You will step on a Broadway stage and pretend to be Elsa or Elphaba or Jasmine and maybe even run into the real thing after the show. You will whisper questions into Dad's ear while watching a run through and visit mom on a lunch break.

When the lights are bright again it will feel bittersweet. There will be less time for crafting, family shows, and long walks. We will miss you both. We might not watch as many episodes of The Great British Baking Show but we will finally have the perfect place to share our brioche loaves and millionaire's shortbread so we don't eat it all ourselves.

When the lights are bright again, we will do what we have always done…make theater. We will do our best to balance the joy of being your Mom and Dad with the opportunity to do the work we always dreamed of. We will long for this time that we have had together and all the ways it fortified us for the times when we have to be apart. We will feel so grateful that we are all healthy and made it through this as a family.

The lights went out on our family of three out in San Francisco and since then we will have become a family of four (five if you count Scout the dog) and moved across the country with a newborn during a pandemic to return home to New York. When the lights are bright again, we will remember all the things we lost along that journey, all the ways we sacrificed to keep each other safe, and all the hard things that had to be done together. **We will still have to do hard things and we will have to do them together, but now we have a lot more practice.**

When the lights are bright again, we will get back to sharing what we love with who we love. Most of all, that is the two of you. Sally, it will be even better than you remember. Wyman, it will be like nothing you've ever seen before.

Love,
Mom and Dad
Lindsay Levine–Casting Director
Ryan Kasprzak–Dance Supervisor
@tapdancekaz | @babyhandsbigdreams
Originally from Fort Myers, FL

Dear Jennifer,

When the lights are bright again, you will cherish being part of a new era in theatre history: **our very own roaring 20s**. For more than a year now, our entire industry has been shut down because of the COVID-19 pandemic. It has been a tragic and challenging time for many reasons, and one of them has been the isolation. Many of us in theatre dreamed of a big life, centered around community. Productions that turn into families, parties that are essentially reunions, walking down a New York City street and running into ten colleagues. Housing together during an out-of-town production, staying up late together during tech, squeezing together on stage for a concert. Collaborating with other humans in actual rooms, meeting and working with heroes, running into friends at auditions and meetings and benefits, readings and opening nights and recording sessions.

As a historian, one thing I know is that great things can come out of heartbreaking times. During the pandemic, I researched and wrote my fourth Untold Stories of Broadway book, and one thing that this book chronicles is the 1982 destruction of five Broadway theaters. I would do anything for a time machine to take me back to 1982 so I could prevent this tragic loss. And yet, while I was writing about it, I discovered just how significantly this event led to the landmarking of almost every other Broadway house. If we had not lost the Morosco, Bijou, old Helen Hayes, Astor and Gaiety four decades ago, we would not have the 41 Broadway theaters we have today.

I have hope and faith that the next era of theatre and of New York City will be filled with similarly unexpected **bright sides, breakthroughs, and progress**. Like so many others, I have desperately missed sharing a space with friends and strangers. Experiencing a story together, live. Collaborating on a moment that will exist forever in collective memory. I am so excited for all of it to return.

The 2020s will forever be shaped by their beginning: a time of extreme hardship and adversity. And out of hardship and adversity, theatre people throughout history have risen and thrived.

To our own roaring 20s!
Jennifer
@jenashtep

> " As a historian, one thing I know is that great things can come out of heartbreaking times. "

Dear Jess,

When the lights are bright again you will weep. Hard. Probably sob is more the right word. It's all felt like a dream. When you and Elliot arrived in La Jolla last March to join E you were expecting to just spend a few weeks, have a lovely mini vacay and then get back to Broadway a month or so later….

A year later the three of you packed up, pulled out and left the little SoCal sanctuary. We were all much more emotional than we thought we'd be. **The amount of life we experienced in that little space is unreal. The heavy, deep grief of loss, our own sickness, the weight and despair over the decimation of our love and livelihood, and yet…**

We were so happy there for the most part.

Elliot has grown in confidence and intellect, E and I both learned new skills, started a business (Ivy & Clarke), & figured out how to remotely record and keep *Mamas Talkin' Loud* going. We were able to eat dinner with Elliot every night and be with her more than we'd ever been in her entire life! We taught her and watched her grow on the daily. She learned to ride a bike and to swim on her own. We adventured together and went camping for the first time. And getting to hang out with lifelong friends we usually see *maybe* once a year, if we're lucky, was a major lift to our souls in a time when those moments were hard to come by.

There's not a doubt in my mind that we would have had a very different experience had we been in the city. By no means did we plan to stay in Cali that long, but man, being in the sunshine, going for hikes, hitting the beach…these made all the difference in how we made it thru the day to day, and endless days when time lost all meaning. In a year when we were scared, lost, untethered, overwhelmingly sad, the gift La Jolla Playhouse gave us is immense and we couldn't be more grateful.

A new chapter is here. These COVID days have taken much, but damn if they didn't give us some magic in the end. The light is getting brighter - you'll be there when they are called to full.

Keep breathing,
Jess
@jessicarush
Originally from Orange, TX

Dear Love for a Singular Sensation,

When the lights are bright again, you will make your debut as a confident, kind, smart, and loving individual. **You will shed your various costumes of insecurities and take center stage as the leading lady in your life.** You will channel all your determination into your new dream of finding love and starting a family. The first act of your life with your professional endeavors was well received, before the unexpected and interruptive intermission for the last couple of years. Now it is time for the curtain to rise on your next act, and all that comes with a true romantic story: musical musings, laughter, probable heartache, courage, understanding, and love. As you push forward on this journey, you will one day find yourself back in a theatre, not only celebrating that the lights are back on, but in the seat next to you is your true love, together embarking upon whatever story is about to be told. You must never forget that you are a singular sensation that is worthy of love and happiness.

Warmest Wishes,
Love for a Singular Sensation
@bessdonoghue
Originally from New York, NY

> Now it is time for the curtain to rise on your next act, and all that comes with a true romantic story: musical musings, laughter, probable heartache, courage, understanding, and love.

To my Theater Community:

When the lights are bright again... It is 6:30pm on a Friday night in late February. It is dark. It is cold, but thankfully not raining. I am sitting socially distanced and masked around a campfire with 9 kids in rural Oregon in a place large enough for a zip code, but too small for a town; primarily united by the school district. What are we doing? Our first rehearsal of the spring musical. Do we know how we will ultimately accomplish our goal to mount a production? Not really. Thankfully, since auditions (held on a porch with the wind blowing rain sideways and everyone blue and shivering), the vaccine roll-out in Oregon has been going full swing, so maybe we will be able to live stream our show or perform outdoors.

I am their theater director, but not their teacher. I have been directing theater here for over 20 years, in a theater program that is entirely voluntary and which brings me unabashed joy. I was a theater professional in NYC in the late 1970s and 1980s, and my day job since has been Family Physician and midwife. **But I have been taught that a task that is too large for one person, can be accomplished by many.** My goal has always been to help actors find the truth in the story, by understanding how it crosses paths with current events. In short, to teach empathy and then to share that generosity of spirit with their fellow actors, and, ultimately in their lives.

When the lights are bright again, myself and my team will be back to applaud every one of the kids and open their home again. **A place that celebrated successes and cried over hurts.** Where we can all be together again, to share the joy that community creates and impart that to our audiences. To feel the electricity between people all sharing the same experience, in real time and together in space.

Katherine Zieman
@katherine_a_zieman
Originally from Peekskill, NY

> " My goal has always been to help actors find the truth in the story, by understanding how it crosses paths with current events. In short, to teach empathy and then to share that generosity of spirit with their fellow actors, and, ultimately in their lives. "

Dear Arian,

When the lights are bright again, be.

It's normal to think about the upheaval and chaos of the last year. The loss of loved ones will always never be forgotten. Those moments of grit and strength must be reflected on. It's important to learn from those tough months of isolation and loneliness, and it's essential to remember the many ways in which your family and friends were there for you. **The euphoria of working again after a long absence should remind you of how blessed you actually are.**

It makes sense that you're thinking toward the future. As you allow yourself to enter into this next phase, continue to daydream. **Imagine a world that's better than what exists now.** Fight for the voiceless, whether they be immigrant children, Black women and men, or the less fortunate. Create opportunities for others to tell their stories through art. Lend a helping hand when a student feels lost or hopeless. Keep pursuing the truth, so you may leave this place better than you found it.

All that said, I ask you: When the lights are bright again, sit back and take it in.

Let it move you and make you laugh.

Tap your feet and clap your hands.

Enjoy the empathy in front of you.

Take in the magic and experience that rare energy with the strangers around you.

Arian, just be.

Loving you as you are,
Arian
@ArianMoayed

> " Keep pursuing the truth, so you may leave this place better than you found it. "

ARIAN MOAYED
Originally from
Tehran, Iran

MAGIC

Dear Conor,

When the lights are bright again, you will find your joy. I know you never imagined this sad time. There isn't a week where you don't see at least two to three shows when you're in the city. Your true happiness is found in the theatre. You love theatre so incredibly much, and without it, you don't know who you are or what you are meant to do right now. But when it comes back, you will find that missing piece of you again! I can't wait for you to be back onstage, wherever that may be, and to feel those lights and hear that orchestra play. You have worked too hard to let your dream be taken away from you. When you get another job, and get to do what you love the most in the world, I know that you will finally feel whole again! Not because of the job, but to be back in the theatre, the one place **that is the closest thing to magic**. When the days get darker and that joy feels so far away, remember 4-year-old Conor seeing his first Broadway show, *Annie*, and his love for this theatre world was sparked. Keep the love for him! I'm so proud of you and everything you have accomplished, you will be back! "The sun'll come out tomorrow!"

Stay Hopeful,
Conor
@conordevoe
Originally from Ocean Isle, NC

> **I miss the energy inside a Broadway house. I miss the intimate feel of a Cabaret space.**

Dear Theresa,

When the lights are bright again, every theatre will explode with so much love and happiness. This concrete playground where many go to refuel their souls will again be vibrant once the nation has been vaccinated, and we begin to eradicate this heinous COVID virus that has decimated so much, including the ARTS community, and claimed so many lives. This virus, as of this writing 2.2.2021, has claimed over 440,000 American lives. I dread the daily reports that have become a normal part of our lives.

I miss the energy inside a Broadway house. I miss the intimate feel of a Cabaret space. I miss the acting, the dancing, the lighting, the voices, the costumes and the staging of a Broadway or Off-Broadway show. I miss that feeling you can only get by participating in live theatre, and your heart explodes with emotion **as the actors share all that is in theirs**. I miss the traffic as I drove in, well not really. Haha.

I look forward to the day when we can all safely gather and share in the spectacular art form of live theatre when the lights are bright again.

Holding onto hope,
Theresa
@Theresapil
Originally from Mineola, Long Island, NY

Dear Leigh-Ann,

When the lights are bright again, you will be one of the first people to go and see them. You will sit in a theater and get to watch magic happen. If it is meant for you, you will get to stand in them and feel their warmth on your face again. Do you remember? They provide a feeling unlike anything else...a feeling that has been lost for over a year. A feeling you miss from deep within your soul. Will that sensation happen again? **Are you still an artist?** Your identity has been questioned over and over during this time. However, when those lights shine bright again, this unrest will be settled, and you will understand that you are, and always will be, an artist.

Holding onto hope,
Leigh-Ann
@Leighesty
Originally from Gorham, ME

Dear Carol,

When the lights are bright again, I HOPE I AM SITTING IN THE DARK! I want to be in a darkened theatre waiting for the lights to come up. I want to be in a theatre waiting to photograph whatever and whoever is on that stage. I want the dark to surround me and watch that one spotlight illuminate a singer/dancer/actor. **I want to watch a slow fade of lights take me to places I never dreamed of before.**

When the lights are bright again, I want to be in the dark.
Carol
@carolroseggphoto
Originally from New York, NY

Dear Jenn

When the lights are bright again, the empty hole in your heart that has formed over the last year will be filled. You haven't known a year over the last 15 years where you didn't see or perform in a show. Just a short 8 weeks before the world changed, you had the opportunity to see two of the most beautiful, moving and thought provoking shows on Broadway that you have ever seen. How special a day it was, traveling to NYC all by yourself, simply because you knew you needed a mental health day away. You had no idea at the time just how important that mental health day would be. Although it has been an extremely tough year away from your friends and fellow community theater performers, you know the lights will shine bright once again for every performer across the world. And I don't think you'll take for granted a single moment on stage ever again. You're starting to cry right now just thinking about that first moment when you step back on a stage or see a show on Broadway again. **The world needs the beauty and magic of live theater.** And one day it will return. For now, hold on to the memories or performances past. And know the lights will be bright again.

For now, keep on singing in the shower and the car to keep your spirits up.
Jenn
@tinydancer616
Originally from Warminster, PA

Dear Susan,

When the lights are bright again, you will be among the first in line to attend live theatre. You will be able to get lost in the stories, the characters, the songs, the incredible voices and the dances. You will be part of an audience again. You will be mesmerized by the talent. You will clap a little harder. You will cheer a little louder. You will stand a little sooner. You will be so grateful to be entertained.

Can't wait.
Susan
Originally from Long Island, NY

Dear Ryan,

When the lights are bright again, you'll enter the theatre as if for the first time. For once, you've arrived early. You save more time now, live life less rushed, less focused on your work. Though you can probably find your seat by yourself you ask for help, knowing more than ever the value of collaboration. You'll take your seat and wait with anticipation, but with less of those old, private anxieties of competition, uncertainty, and fear. You'll check your watch (you've finally accepted you should turn your phone off more), and think that no matter when the show begins, even if it's a few minutes late, even if it feels too late, it will begin exactly when it's ready to. Things happening exactly when they're supposed to is a thought that's been on your mind a lot over the last year.

As you wait, you'll consciously look around you to the faces you might not have noticed before. The other people sharing this experience with you, those sitting in front of you, behind you, and beside you. But just as this fills you with a mix of heavy feelings, someone asks if you would mind switching seats with them, your preferred seat on the aisle. And you'll become aware then that you tend to always get the good seats, and today you gladly trade with someone who needs it more. Someone else enters the row and you stand to let them get by—you know better now the space you occupy and the space you still have to create.

You'll take in this audience of theater queens and fellow artists and the fans and stans and you will remember that in this community, in your community, there is still so much to be done. Enough work to fill a thousand theaterfuls. You're telling yourself you are only one person alone in one theatre, but your husband takes your hand and the house lights fade (you forgot you were waiting and suddenly it all feels too soon) until everything goes black.

And in this darkness you've found so much comfort in, you will be reminded of what was lost and what had to be found. And you will give yourself over to that higher power of theatre for the evening, until the long, magical moment is over. Over, and the lights are bright again.

Ryan
@ryanscottoliver

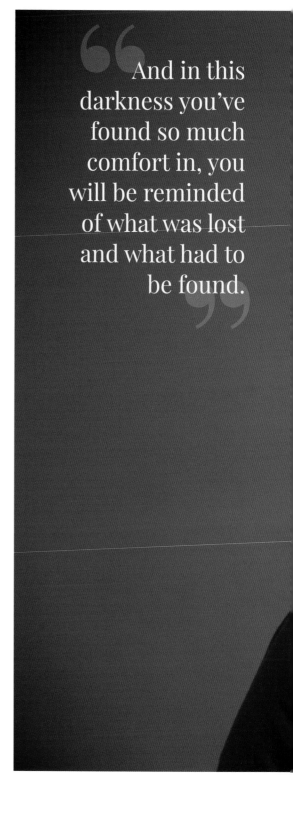

> *And in this darkness you've found so much comfort in, you will be reminded of what was lost and what had to be found.*

RYAN SCOTT OLIVER
Originally from
Pasadena, CA

Dear Ryan,

When the lights are bright again, I pray that we really use the things this pandemic and this time away from live theatre have taught us:

May we never again take for granted that electric buzz in the air as the sounds of ushers showing the audience to their seats, pre-show cocktails being poured at the bar, tourists stuffing their shopping bags under their feet and opening up their Playbills, and the slight hum of the orchestra tuning meld together to create that magical, infectious spark of attending LIVE theatre!

May we always treasure the ability to sit in close proximity to others and share in the communal experience of watching a captivating story unfold before us. May we cherish hearing 1,500 spectators collectively laugh at the same joke or that beautiful moment in each show where a hush comes over the audience and you could cut the silence with a knife.

May we appreciate the seemingly insignificant, but utterly beautiful, moments that happen when working together to put on a show. The dresser that zips you quickly into your costume and gives you a sip of water before sending you back on stage, the sound person who adjusts the placement of your body microphone and hands you an extra piece of toupee tape to make sure it stays in place, the stage manager who reminds you to check your props before they call places, the warm-ups and stretching sessions before the show, quick moments of dressing room chatter, sharing inside jokes with other castmates and crew members, and then, the ultimate thrill of stepping out onto the stage, as the lights blind you for that one quick moment before the thrill and adrenaline of the performance sweep you away. Before you know it, you've reached the end of the show, and you're bowing before a crowd who are standing on their feet and showering you with applause. **Once the curtain closes, the magic gets put to bed, only to come back to life the next night.**

> May we demonstrate love, compassion, kindness, and care for one another and build each other up, rather than tearing each other down.

May we also use our time away from the theatre to rethink, retool, and reimagine what theatre should be, and may we come back ready to be champions of dramatic change in our artform and our industry. May we yearn to see more authentic representation on stage. May we celebrate people of different sizes, abilities, sexual orientations, ethnicities, races, and cultural backgrounds. May we give a voice to the voiceless. May we focus more on the creative and communal aspects of our work, and far less on the business aspects. May we demonstrate love, compassion, kindness, and care for one another and build each other up, rather than tear each other down.

May we all work together to build a better theatre community and a better, stronger artform.

But above all, may we never forget our time without the magic of live theatre!

Holding on to hope,
Ryan
@RyScobes
Originally from Murfreesboro, TN

Dear Lisa,

When the lights are bright again, I'll still be promising to bring my daughter Audrey to a "Show!" as she demands 50 times a day. Because, let's face it, she'd see a show every day, if she could. She's so lucky that I work in the theater. She gets to see shows much more than the average person! But it's never enough for her.

She's 15 but doesn't understand why there are no shows. "Where are the actors?" she asks repeatedly. As if I'm not depressed enough seeing all my friends unemployed, and having my own work hours cut drastically. As if it isn't painful enough that my entire industry, my livelihood, my life's work, has been shut down. I have to be reminded of it every fifteen minutes with Audrey's incessant questions.

And, from somewhere deep within me, I have to find the patience to explain it again and again. "There are no shows right now." "The actors are waiting for the shows to come back, too." "Soon. Soon there will be shows again. We just have to be patient."

So, until that time, I'm stuck hearing Audrey watch parts of her favorite musicals on YouTube: *Mamma Mia* and *Joseph and the Amazing Technicolor Dreamcoat*. They are great shows, but AUGH – I'm getting so sick of them! If I have to hear, "Go, go, go Joseph" one more time…

When the lights are bright again, we will both be so happy. Until then, we have to be patient. What other choice do we have?

Love,
Lisa
@lisapattersonbcp
Originally from Princeton, NJ

> This is my life and my career, and I'll never stop trying because performing makes me happier than anything else.

Dear Michaela,

When the lights are bright again, that empty, missing feeling in the pit of your gut will finally cease. You'll walk across Times Square to the Delacorte or the Broadway or the Stephen Sondheim or the Helen Hayes, and you'll feel that same nervous excitement you always felt before you saw a show, but this time will feel like the very first time. This time will be exactly the same feeling as when you were eight years old, and you saw *Beauty and the Beast*, and you walked out of the theatre feeling that electric energy of New York and Broadway, and passed thousands of other strangers who had no idea that this is what you live for. **That theatre has always felt like therapy to you, from that moment on, and that sitting anonymously in a crowd watching something unfold in front of you that feels true and real and happy and sad is how you understand the world better.** Living in these imaginary circumstances with characters always having the right words to say and the right way to say it has always made me envious, maybe that's why I love to do it so much. Escaping into a world that feels completely separate yet totally connected to yourself. I miss the cool, plush velvet seats, I miss the tiny bathrooms in the older theaters, the old crown molding and gorgeous ceiling murals, the larger than life curtain, the decorated and intricate set pieces and costumes, the well-rehearsed and excited actors, but most of all, I miss that connection between audience and company. I miss feeling a part of something bigger than myself, being part of a large scale machine that started every night at 8 and didn't stop until past 10. I miss the pounding of applause in my ears, and I miss hollering and cheering for the cast, even when the people around me would give me funny side glances. Broadway is a big brotherhood, inviting and inclusive, and, if anything, I'm grateful for this pause if only for the reminder that this means everything to me. This is my life and my career, and I'll never stop trying because performing makes me happier than anything else. I can't wait until I see that first marquee all lit up again–I'll be waiting here.

Best,
Michaela
@michaelamarymor
Originally from Novato, CA

Dear Jim,

May I start by saying that you're looking especially fetching today?

When the lights are bright again, I know you will remember the dark days of the past year. Life has ups and downs, and it's the down times that make the good ones so much more golden. Being locked in an apartment for over a year with no outside stimulation, and none of the people and activities you hold most dear was a complete drag. No singing and swinging in chic little boites. No kvelling over or applauding great entertainment. No laughing with pals over post-show dinners at Joe Allen. No traveling to far-flung cities to celebrate show biz. These are a few of your favorite things, and I know you've missed the hell out of them.

But get ready… I'm going to tell you something I admire about you. I know. A rarity. I'm proud that you, and so many like you, not only survived this insanity–but flourished. When the chips were down, you continued to do what you love most, thanks to the kindness of many. You took your Party to the interwebs and entertained the masses. I know better than anyone you did it as much for yourself, but we'll keep that to ourselves. The point is you got moving and made something happen. **It made you continue to feel like a vital New Yorker, which is about the best thing anyone could want to be.**

As the world returns to some semblance of normalcy, a bit of the past year's misery will fade, and that's OK. You don't need to drag that stuff around with you. But know that I'm watching you and cheering your joy in life, your optimism, and your relentless dreams.

Yours,
You
@jimcaruso1

JIM CARUSO
Originally from
Pittsburgh, PA

Dear Kaitlyn,

When the lights are bright again, you will find yourself again. Not your sense of purpose, reason to live or fulfillment of fate, but you will get to do the thing that gives you the most joy and confidence. That feeling of doing what you have wanted and waited your whole life to do. The dream job that you finally obtained, got a taste of, and your passions of performing realized. Not just the dreams though, but the professional goals you set for yourself. Knowing you are a professional, an artist with a finely crafted and honed skill that deserves the well-paying money she makes. Skills that you spent your whole life and savings on.

No, I am not going to "find something new." See above. No, I am not going to switch mediums. The reason I started performing is the reason I still perform. Something special drew me to theatre, a distinct feeling and memory. A story that happens time and time again and, though it felt special to me, it wasn't uniquely mine. I was that little girl who had no knowledge of who she could be until she made eye contact with a performer in a live production and saw herself doing that very same thing. It was captivating. And now every show I do, I pay that inspiration forward. **There is something tangible, a kinetic energy, that is unexplainable between an audience and a performer.** It's not the individual artistry, the fame or praise during my final bow that I love, but the experience of live, collaborative theatre and shared empathy. It gives me perspective and keeps me grounded. It lets me be fully and unashamedly myself.

I knew that. I knew how good I had it. I didn't need some divine intervention or lesson telling me that. I miss my *Mean Girls* tour cast and show tremendously, but mostly I miss the opportunity of being able to be my true self...where everything fell away and I was truly content. And even without it, I have found ways to find contentment. **I wish, but I don't beg.** I have been blessed to not get the virus or have anyone taken from me. I ache for those who have, and I let that gratefulness sink in everyday. At the end of all this, I have a lot to be grateful for. So I wait and wait patiently. I wait filled with hope and excitement for what's on the other side. I haven't actually been under the lights of Broadway, but I know one day I will be.

To a brighter tomorrow,
Kaitlyn Louise Smith
@kaitlynlsmitty
Originally from St. Louis, MO

> "I miss my *Mean Girls* tour cast and show tremendously, but mostly I miss the opportunity of being able to be my true self...where everything fell away and I was truly content. And even without it, I have found ways to find contentment."

Dear PJ,

When the lights are bright again, you will cherish the magic. This year has taught you many lessons, but **it has not taken away your dreams**. Keep shining bright, stay true to yourself, and share your love with the world.

Love,
PJ
@pjdigaetano
Originally from Spring Hill, FL

> "We do it because: We love the Theatre. We love great theatre experiences. We want to share them. We want to uplift people."

Dear Corey Brunish,

When the lights are bright again, it will all come flooding back. It will fill the cells of our bodies with tingling elation. We will feel as though we are floating as we walk. A spring in our step will be an understatement. We will recall in visceral terms why we do what we do. As a producer, it is often suspected that we do it for the money, or the awards, but I think this is shortsighted. To say "We don't do it for the awards or money" sounds like a questionable philosophy. And yet. When we examine our motives, and why we truly, deep down do it, the answer becomes much more clear. We do it because: We love the Theatre. We love great theatre experiences. We want to share them. We want to uplift people. We want them to feel better on the way out of the theatre than when they went in. **We want to add to the global conversation.** We want to employ theatre practitioners (as many as 200 per production, all told, on stage and off). We want to do even the smallest thing to make the world a better, more pleasant place to live. We want to bring people together and deliver a positive message to all. We believe in the cooperative effort of making living art and in the audience as key participants in that creation. If, in the pursuit of these things, someone wants to pat us on the back and say "job well done" and "keep going" that's fine too. We appreciate it. So much the better. Awards aren't why we do it. But it does feel good to hear "Thank You" now and again. And by the way–Thank You for attending live theatre!

Love and Light!
Corey Brunish
@coreybrunish
Originally from Los Angeles, CA

Dear Brooke,

When the lights are bright again... you will be, too. **Broadway credit or not, this is your family**. This is your home and no one can deny that you have made yourself a part of it. When the lights went dark, so did your world. Years of onlooking, self doubt, and the desire turned sickness of wanting to be "in it" so bad… and…here you are. You made it. A community, a world, a dream that you always strove for. It took having it all taken away for you to clearly see just how "in it" you are. How lucky you are to have felt what was, and to have stuck it out in times of darkness and unknown. When the lights are bright again.. you will be here and ready for whatever will be. Don't be scared or afraid of not being "ready" to return to what was, because you have evolved. **Continue to make your own art without reason, without permission, without question.** Deep down you know, you always have. Continue to open your arms wide for all of the magic this city reveals to those brave enough to look for it, to see it. You never know what will happen when you step outside of your door. Look up at the sky and breathe in all that life has to offer. Continue to tell your stories, follow through, say yes to the things and people who set you on fire, and always remember to get back up. You are resilient with your reckless heart and that…that is what you will be remembered for. Trust in your heart that you are where you belong and when the lights are bright again, and they will be, it will be time to let your light shine bright as well.

Believe unconditionally. When you let your heart lead the way, you will radiate, and you never know who you may be a lighthouse for.

As I sit here and write this to you, I think of *Damn Yankees* National Tour January 1996. "You Gotta Have Heart."

Five-year-old B sitting in that seat looking up at the stage with wonder, awe and a tiny inkling inside of what could be would be proud. You are a glimmering Quasar.

Celebrate what makes you special and never stop sharing it… because that is magic.

Endless love and forgiveness,
Brooke
@Bsing20
Originally from Houston, TX

RICK MIRAMONTEZ
Originally from
Los Angeles, CA

Dear Rick,

When the lights are bright again...

You will never fall asleep in the theater again.

You will never complain about having to see a show again.

You will never leave at intermission again.

You will be grateful for every performer, every musician, every creator, every technician and every stagehand who've poured their souls into making magic upon the stage for your enjoyment. It is your privilege to witness their work, and you will never take it for granted again.

You will never, ever fall asleep in the theater again.

Yours,
Rick
@rickmiramontez1

Dear Barbara,

When the lights are bright again–Who knows what the other side of this time will look like? How can you know when the battle with a shapeshifter is over?

What I do know is, for a year, the only people I venture out to meet for socially-distant coffee are my theatre friends. Sitting outside, bundled in jackets and masks, drinking through straws. We have more eye contact than usual because your friends don't quite resemble themselves when masks conceal half their face.

We talk about how bizarre, how surreal life has become. The suddenness of all this, expecting it was a pattern of interruption for a month or two, then seasons go by, everything changing. The tragedy of so many deaths…

And then mutations. That's when you realize there is not going to be an – Again.

However this ends, whatever comes next, will be different.

Why are the bonds across theatre so strong? Because we all witnessed the magic of theatre – we made it happen together.

Writing plays, reading, planning, casting, production logistics, acting, front of house, concessions. The panic of tech week before every show opens. Waking up at 3 a.m., knowing this just isn't ready, and yet, when the lights go down on opening night, through some alchemy, the performance comes together.

What now? Before all this, National Theatre Live filmed plays – masterful productions like *War Horse* – with a front row seat for the price of a movie ticket. But that took a budget to film – and would it have that effect on a laptop?

Your role becomes audience.

You can finally see plays of Adrienne Kennedy streamed from Round House Theater. Ten minute plays filmed outside kind of work. You end up streaming a lot of independent films. And while you haven't combated the inertia of "all the time in the world" you now have to finish plays – for when the lights are bright – every time you start to see a light at the end of this tunnel…

The day job part of your brain kicks in – the part immersed in numbers and patterns and trends – and all you see is something more ominous looming, the shapeshifter on the horizon, and a shadow over the light.

We're like magicians, we'll figure out new ways to produce theater, but there may not be an "Again."

Barbara
Originally from Baltimore County, MD

> "Why are the bonds across theatre so strong? Because we all witnessed the magic of theater – we made it happen together."

Dear Lauren,

When the lights are bright again… You will cherish the miracles

Magic is woven; look all around

The waves that carry you out of darkness, also carry you home

The ashes turn into stories, and the stories are determined by you

If you look hard enough you might see that all you need is each other

Let the tears flood and fill your life; coming and going constantly

Mourn for the things you have lost and celebrate the memories to come

Memories like the roaring sound of applause, the vibrations shaking the floor

The shining heroes on the stage who have come to share a story

Stories of triumph, loss, bravery, and vulnerability

Stories that make my brain boil or cry with endearment

Stories that have made me who I am today

So when the lights are bright again, I will be ready

And as the moment comes when the lights are dimmed, the audience gets quiet

The silence more overwhelming than ever

The moment before the show starts, the magic dust that overcomes the fans

Before the first instrument is played;

I will be ready.
Lauren
@laurendietert
Originally from Houston, TX

> Memories like
> the roaring
> sound of
> applause, the
> vibrations
> shaking the
> floor
>
> The shining
> heroes on the
> stage who have
> come to share
> a story

Dear Alia,

When the lights are bright again...the fast walk through Times Square, the check-in with the box office, the murmur of the audience settling into their seats, the silence right before the first chord plays as the curtain rises, and the exuberance of that singular connection between the cast on stage and the people in their seats is what I cannot wait for on the other side. **That feeling that this magic is all fleeting – could all be lost – was replaced with the love this community has expressed in so many ways during this pandemic.** I love this community for mourning so much loss together, for reaching out to stay connected, for pivoting to create in the virtual world, and for seeking ways to make Broadway better when we reopen.

Filled up with the compassion my family, friends, producing partner, Women Independent Producers Group and Broadway Advocacy Coalition have shared over the past 15 months, I have no doubt that we, the theater community, are taking a quantum leap forward. This pandemic may have kept us out of the theater just long enough for the racial reckoning to compel us to examine and redesign systems that have discriminated, alienated, and disadvantaged our members and audiences.

My dream for the theater community coming out of this pause is for it to be a leader in the conversation around diversity, equity and inclusion with intentional actions to make the industry systemically inclusive, nurturing and equitable for its members, safe for its members and audiences, and continuously expanding. Front Row Productions will continue to champion work that meets these criteria and asks the theater community to do the same.

With love,
Alia
@aliajharvey

> " I love this community for mourning so much loss together, for reaching out to stay connected, for pivoting to create in the virtual world... "

PRESENT

Dear Sami,

When the lights are bright again, you'll feel the rush of theatre magic. The rush of running a Broadway show (or any show for that matter) is one of the best feelings in the world. I used to think I knew anxiety, learning a new track for the first time in a theatre of people I didn't know. What if I made a mistake? What if a zipper gets stuck? What if I'm late or get lost? What if people don't like me? Will the show have to stop if I am bad at my job? But, the post-performance adrenaline rush is the most incredible thing I've ever felt. I remember my first night at *Les Mis*, the first Broadway show I worked on. I left the theatre, and walking through Times Square, cried on the phone to my mother about how overwhelmed and terrified I was. There was no way I would remember every costume piece, and change, and actor. The night I successfully ran a track by myself, I left the theatre and felt like I could fly. Sami, you will feel that again. **The accomplishment of doing your job well.** Of leaving a stage door and seeing all the audiences clamoring to see the actors. I love being a crew member and sneaking out of the theatre like a kept secret. Someone audiences don't know, but can tell they love their job. One of the lucky ones who gets past the stage door. Sami, you will feel that again. You will feel joy and frustration, love and anger, too much coffee and not enough sleep, too many lost buttons and broken shoes. But most importantly, you will feel it all again. You will sing along to the music, get to work with gorgeous costumes, and make the change, and remember the hat and the shoes, and dance off-stage, and enjoy every moment with the Broadway family. You will get to witness history again, on stage from the wings, and that's a pretty great view.

Keep your dreams and stitches strong,
Sami
Originally from Columbus, OH

> **But hopefully this year reminds you of empathy and patience for when we are back in full swing.**

Dearest SM AshleyRoseGal,

When the lights are bright again…you will shed little tears of relief that include every possible emotion. You will be happy to have the responsibilities to care for our peers in person on a daily basis. We know you've missed the joy, the quick thinking, the wit to problem solve at the toss of a coin. But hopefully this year reminds you of empathy and patience for when we are back in full swing. Just think of all of the sunsets you would have missed without pausing this year now that you'll be in the dark again backstage forevermore. Let the year fade away gracefully, know that you are back where you belong, remember the lessons, and cherish how lucky you are (and have always been) to be right here.

Love,
SM AshleyRoseGal
@AshleyRoseGal
Originally from Garden City, Long Island, NY

Dear Mimi,

When the lights are bright again, you will put on a show for all the children you've been singing Broadway lullabies to, so they could get through this difficult time. So they will know that even though we all go through difficult times, they are loved. You will travel and get together with family and friends on a regular basis. You will always remember to tell them how much you love them and value their place in your life and the world; **THAT THEY MATTER**. You will be kinder to yourself and tell yourself that **YOU MATTER.** You will remember your many moments of reflection during the pandemic and continue your theater career with newfound conviction and dedication. You will forgive those you love for all their crazy behavior that upset you because we lived through a pandemic that killed millions of people. You will meet and share your life with a special man who loves and respects you.

Much love,
Mimi
@meemsbessette
Originally from Ridgefield, CT

> " You will travel and get together with family and friends on a regular basis. "

Dear Kelsee,

When the lights are bright again, and a semblance of hustle and bustle in our new world has begun, may you never forget just how badly you missed it all. The good, the bad, the exciting, the frustrating, and yes, the downright ugly. May you never forget how determined you remained to return to the stage; to recover in tandem with an industry that has given you everlasting love and purpose. May you never forget indulging in recordings by the fallible bootlegger, while aching with tears in your eyes for the live theatre experience to once again be a reality. The simple and humbling realization that a phone in a theatre – a concept that normally made you hotheaded – has now provided great comfort and joy, as it reminded you that a phone and its proprietor once inhabited a theatre at all.

May you never forget just how badly you yearned to move forward. Human beings are creatures of habit, yet we end up longing for change. **Creative beings refuse to idle.** We smash creative goals, try new things, and leverage with fears of failure and/or success. We crave newness, as with the bloom and fall of the calendar's seasons. Too much constance makes us tired, cue: dissatisfaction and an ever-looming, cyclical feeling of "never enough."

When the lights are bright again, may you always remember how this catastrophic time made space for your discoveries - both personal and worldly - to invigorate and heal you. Make peace with the version of yourself that you have become, for without the pandemic's many faults and halts, this very version of you would have never been able to exist. May this lead you gracefully into the future with new eyes, new ears, new intentions, and surely… a greater appreciation for hugs.

Jonathan Larson's "no day but today" carried you head-first into this pandemic. Clichés aside, honor the necessity of that phrase. Here's to all the things you did, all the things you're going to do, and all the things you'll simply never do, thanks to the many unsought, bittersweet gifts of this bewildering time.

Love always,
Kelsee
@kelseesweigard
Originally from Harrisburg, PA

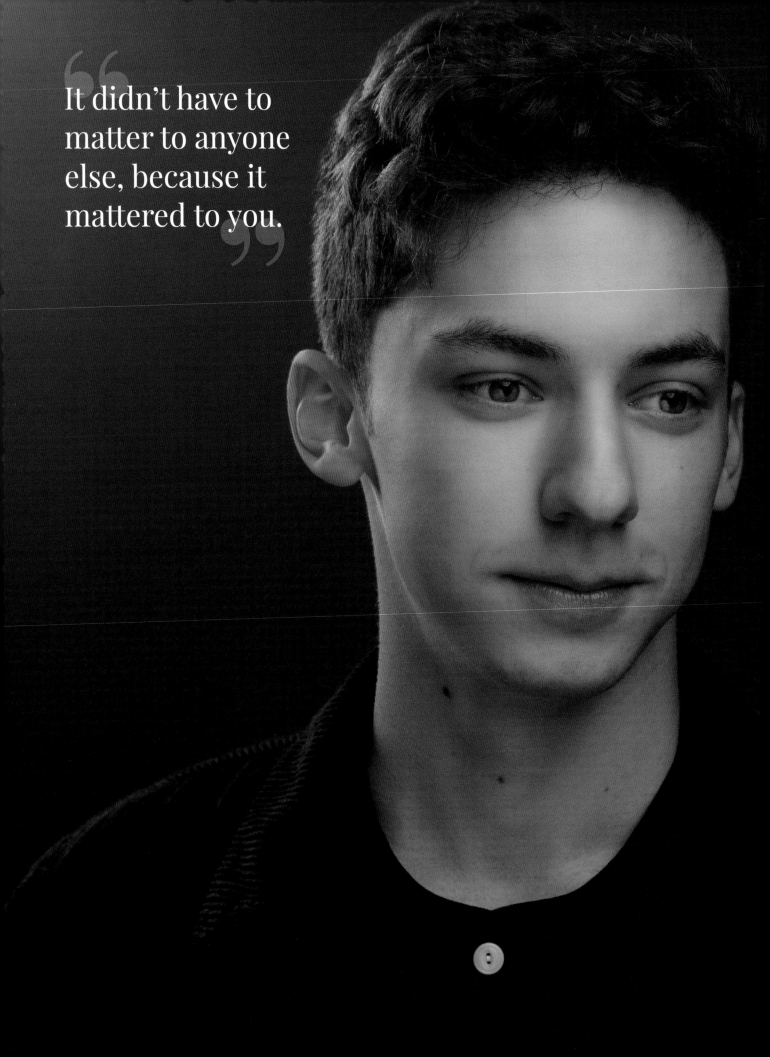

"It didn't have to matter to anyone else, because it mattered to you."

ANDREW BARTH FELDMAN
Originally from
Long Island, NY

Dear Andrew,

When the lights are bright again, they'll find you different than you were.

Everyone has always told you, "if you could do anything else, do it." Every young actor hears that just about every day. You tried anything else: debate, coding, sports, chess...you couldn't do anything else. You were and are very bad at the majority of things. You had one love. That's why you're here.

You went through the most difficult, tragic year of your life, had about two weeks of eating pizza and going on roller coasters and living a normal teenage-hood, and then went through the second most difficult year of your life. That first year, when everything fell apart, you spent your time healing under those lights. When everything fell apart again, there were no lights at all. So you lit some for yourself. You had to do something just to stay mentally afloat, and you couldn't do anything else, so you didn't. You brought people together, raised money for charity, created, wrote, performed. You did what you've always done. It didn't have to matter to anyone else, because it mattered to you.

You didn't know you could do all that. But, now, I can very clearly see that you always could have. And that anyone can. And that there will be many, many more times in your life where you're faced with something that you believe you alone cannot overcome. And that there will be another you, days or weeks or months or years later, that can very clearly see that you always could have.

I'm really, really proud of you. And when the lights are bright again, they will be, too.

Sincerely,
Andrew
@andrewbfeldman_

Dear Jonalyn,

When the lights are bright again,

Love the joy. Love with your whole heart.

Remember the ache of absence you felt.

Remember the fun times with family. The relaxation. The self healing. The connections. The students and lives reached.

Remember to accept yourself.

Remember the curveball that got thrown, and that you kept moving.

Enjoy the time onstage and off. The joy of a strong handhold in a lift. Every high-five and hug, and the little moments in-between.

When the lights are bright again,

I'm going to breathe. To love each performance, rehearsal, audition, class.

I'll know that sometimes the train feels like it's running away from you, but even when you think it's all stopped, it's still chugging along.

Remember how much you learned to live for the RIGHT NOW, when even a month ahead was unsure. And KEEP living for NOW. After all, that's why its called the present. It's a gift.

When the lights are bright again,

Not everything will be solved. It was never perfect, and it will never be perfect. Remember your mission statement. Be a part of a better industry. Of a loving industry. Of a joyful and excited industry.

It took a full stop to make you dream bigger. Keep dreaming bigger. Dream big for you. Dream big for your friends.

When the lights are bright again,

Our family will be reunited. The family we knew we had, but didn't realize how much we needed.

When the lights are bright again…

Keep moving forward.

Who knows what will happen. You didn't sign up for stability.

You show up for love.
Jonalyn
@jksaxer
Originally from Agoura Hills, CA

> And KEEP living for NOW. After all, that's why its called the present. It's a gift.

> Our family will be reunited. The family we knew we had, but didn't realize how much we needed.

> "Be kinder to yourself and live in the moment. When the lights are bright again you'll shine in your own way, as you've always pushed to do."

Dear Ben,

When the lights are bright again, you'll keep trying your best. You've missed it, don't let your apathy tell you otherwise. The time away has killed the dreams inside of you and it's up to you to resuscitate them. Do not let the tunnel vision of needing to survive, nor the apathy of disconnection sway you from the craft that makes you feel whole. When it's back, **remember that you're good enough to be in every space you occupy; remember what you wrote**:

> "I miss theatre because I miss going to see friends in shows. I miss auditioning for my wildest dreams. I miss throwing my proverbial penny behind my back in the Trevi fountain that could be my future. I miss the theatre as a space for experimental explosive devices. I miss being entertained by something writ four scores prior to my attendance. I miss my blood flow shifting through character development and my eyes darting to whomever holds the energy of the room. I miss my purpose."

Be kinder to yourself and live in the moment. When the lights are bright again, you'll shine in your own way, as you've always pushed to do. Stay thankful for the ones with whom you've journeyed.

With Love,
Ben Salus
@bensalus
Originally from Jenkintown, PA

Dear Danny,

When the lights are bright again, allow yourself a moment to feel the joy that is living out your dreams. My wish for you is to be fully present and truly see what you've been missing.

May you see the people who surround you every day as more than co-workers. They are your shipmates who have weathered this storm alongside you. They are your partners in grief. They have called, texted, and FaceTimed to check in on you, sometimes daily. They sent you letters, funny photos, and birthday gifts. They forgave you for declining their Zoom invitations. They supported your new hobbies and interests, and cheered you on from afar. **They shared their strength with you when they barely had enough for themselves.** They reminded you that this, too, shall pass. They lived in their own fears and worries and still saved energy to comfort you. These people care for you like you're one of their own, because you are.

May you see the theatre itself as a sacred vessel. Time spent there is a true gift. That place has given you lifelong friendships, wise mentors, and memories that always bring you light in darkness. With every coming performance, honor those who have come before you, and those who would be there if they were able. Bring them with you when you enter the stage door. May your places calls heard throughout the building always invoke your passion for theatre and remind you to never take it for granted.

Remember the profundity of your art form. It heals people. These are the stories, plays, musicals, and people that have carried you through your own sea of grief. The words, voices, and music filled your home and lifted your spirit when you didn't have it in you to even get dressed in the morning (or afternoon). The healing power that your work wields is stronger than you'd ever imagined and needed now more than ever.

When the lights are bright again, enjoy the ride. The long hours, stress, and paperwork are all part of the journey. Welcome the pencil sharpening, taping out, three-hole punching, recording, reporting, and sometimes over-communicating with open arms. Be grateful for the problems left for you to solve.

Love,
Danny
Originally from North Riverside, IL

Dear Eden

When the lights are bright again, you will be brand new. You will have your feet on the ground. You will know your worth. You will have expanded so far beyond ever having to make yourself small again. You made it through a dark time without having set foot on a stage, or embodying a character, and look at where you are. You are thriving. It took you losing everything you thought you needed to survive. To finally be unapologetically you. I'm proud of you. I love you.

Shine on my love,
Eden
@EdenEspinosa

> " You made it through a dark time without having set foot on a stage, or embodying a character, and look at where you are. "

EDEN ESPINOSA
Originally from
Orange County, CA

Dear Andrew,

> **This moment in time, this shared experience that we all have had is incredibly unique in that we all had to do what was best for us at the time, and for you, you placed your love for theatre, your passion for theatre, your calling, in a box and set it aside, because the prospect of never performing again was too heartbreaking to face.**

When the lights are bright again, I'm not sure what you'll do. It's easy to hypothesize what might happen, but we all know that putting unrealistic expectations on ourselves is fruitless. The truth is, I think in this past year I've become numb… numb because, after years of being blessed to work regularly, it had been several months since you last performed when the lights on Broadway and in theaters across the country went out indefinitely. When that announcement came, I think you suppressed any sadness you might have felt, and any sense of belonging to the theatre community faded, which led you to become distant and disconnected from the community you once called home. This moment in time, this shared experience that we all have had, is incredibly unique in that we all had to do what was best for us at the time. And for you, you placed your love for theatre, your passion for theatre - your calling - in a box and set it aside, because the prospect of never performing again was too heartbreaking to face. Having spent the last decade performing, I was finally faced with a question that I had spent the past 10 years avoiding… **"who are you when you are not performing?"**

The short answer is, you're still you, Andrew. You are surrounded by a beautiful, supportive family, happy parents, happy husband, gracious friends, and your apartment in Hamilton Heights is still your sanctuary. Your heart is just as full now, regardless of whether or not you are onstage. Perhaps this serves as a reminder that whether or not you "booked the show" or have a show to go back to when the lights are bright again, you are still incredibly loved and have so much love to give, and that is something a pandemic can't change. While you've been taking this time away to focus on Graduate School studies in Arts Administration, you're further securing a place in the arts for yourself for the rest of time…whether or not you're performing, you've taken this time to pledge allegiance to the arts in whatever capacity you can be most useful, and for that, I applaud you.

I applaud this entire community for staying positive, staying creative, and exploring other things. Whatever your journey was during this time, when the lights are bright again, I truly hope my theatre community welcomes me back with open arms, because this reunion will undoubtedly be joyful and emotional. I remember after 9/11 when Bernadette Peters led the entire Broadway community in a rousing rendition of "New York, New York" in Times Square. My teenage heart was sent into orbit and I still get emotional thinking about it. Now at 34, I am starting to feel a similar pang of emotion. I guess I'm no longer numb. What a moment that will be for our community, not just on Broadway, but across the country… **"start spreadin' the news…"**

With a good deal of love,
Andrew Eckert
@Andrewreckert
Originally from Harrisburg, PA

Dear Ali,

When the lights are bright again, the light inside you will shine again. While your career in theater does not define you, it brings you a joy like nothing else in this world. Class is your therapy. Your escape. Your celebration. Rehearsal rooms and stages are your home. Casts and creative teams are your family. You've laughed and cried in every major NYC rehearsal studio and hallway. You've given your heart and soul to developing new works and revisiting old ones.

When NYC shut down, your show kept on rehearsing until the last possible second. We held on until there was nothing left to hold on to. You had multiple jobs in the pipeline and were looking forward to a year of working with some of your favorite people. Your best friend made a point to come see you on your lunch break on that final day. She knew what was coming, even if you were still in denial.

This break has been a roller coaster. You've experienced some beautiful highs and some crippling lows. Still, you are strong. You seized new and different opportunities. You learned to have days where nothing was planned. You quarantined with family and cooked healthy meals. You raised a puppy! But you are ready to get back. And when you do, you will savor every moment like never before. Putting on rehearsal clothes. The feel of your feet in character shoes. The first notes of an overture. A laugh from an audience member. The sound of applause. Taking your first bow. It gives me chills just thinking about it and I cannot wait to experience it all again.

Keep searching for the lights. They will come back on.
Ali
@AliSolomonNY
Originally from Manorville, NY

Dear Karen,

WHEN THE LIGHTS ARE BRIGHT AGAIN….Your head is gonna explode with joy! You will be overwhelmed with emotion when you sing your first note in front of a real, in-person audience. You are going to be wildly happy…. Because you are home again with your family of artists! Please remember that feeling. **Remember to always enjoy this ride that is art….that is LIFE!**

This past year, your Mom died a week before her 96th birthday, you dealt with some health issues, and learned new skills, (yes, those weekly FB "giglets" have made technology less frightening! And, very impressively, you learned how to close your collapsible backdrop in less than 4 hours!!). You have been dreaming of the day when you would hear laughter and applause IN PERSON! And, yes, even some sniffling because you shared a beautiful ballad with your audience. And yes, you will get hugs again!

Many times, you were just too competitive and too driven! You forgot to enjoy the moment. From this day forward, remember to love the moment! Appreciate all the chaotic, complicated beauty that is around you. All the talented, crazy souls you get to work with. Learn from them. **Time is so precious, Karen. Listen, and make every moment count!**

Always,
Karen
Originally from Jackson Heights, NY

> **Many times, you were just too competitive and too driven! You forgot to enjoy the moment. From this day forward, remember to love the moment!**

Dear Clyde,

When the lights are bright again, you will re-enter a stage forever changed. Boards further creased, but more broken in than broken. Although your experience has been uniquely yours, you will take comfort in the common trials of a thousand communities. You will have found your way through a global shutdown much longer than the initially anticipated "few weeks." You will have treaded water, risen & fallen 20 times over. This time will add a chapter, then another, and another.... You will face dark days of unexplained loss and thank the sun for the life very much existing in and around you and others. You'll have watched your son quite literally grow. You'll hold your wife's hand through love, laughter, uncertainty, pain and lottery winning elation. On some days, you'll wonder if and when you'll ever be able to get back on a stage, yet immediately start to miss the endless amounts of life you've been able to live during this "Pause." Ultimately, you and a billion others will experience a reset. Suddenly having so much taken away will hold a magnifying glass over what is really important. But what about the Theatre? Is it your playground? Is it merely a way for you to earn a living? This time has tested your Artist vs. Family experiment. After all this world has recently endured, what significance does it still hold? Although you will have had the time to ask yourself a myriad of questions, you will not have had enough to put all the pieces back together. With that, there are a few things that will become clear... Being in a room with other people and sharing our stories is one of the most basic yet fundamental parts of the human experience. You've missed it. The world will need it more than ever. To cry together. To laugh together. To show us that we have so much more in common than that which divides us. So yeah, when the lights are bright again, your storytelling will be stronger, rested and loaded with the sharpest jazz hands you ever did see!

Clyde
@Alvesface

CLYDE ALVES
Originally from
Brampton, Ontario,
Canada

ROBYN HURDER
Originally from
Windham, ME

HUDSON

Dear Robyn,

When the lights are bright again, you will be too. There is no denying that a certain spark has dimmed inside you this past year. Don't worry, it's still there, it's just resting as a glowy little ember that occasionally spurts out a flicker every now and then. Look at your wrist Robyn. Remember why you got those stars. Nothing, not even a horrific pandemic, can take away your true special sparkle. But BOY has it tried. How many times have you looked up to the sky and asked God, Universe...whatever you want to call it, "What else? What else are you going to throw at me this year? How strong do you think I actually am?" The past 13 months have been a test. A test for what? I'm not sure. I think I'll find out the real meaning further down the road. Right now, I'm still sad. I'm still confused. You are a person who needs to know the answer immediately. There aren't answers as to why people are taken from us too soon. Nick. I think about him and Amanda multiple times a day still. Every day. My soul drops and my eyes burn. He should be here. My

mother in law, Teresa. She should be here. I still can't believe she's gone. The most soul crushing experience I have ever felt and continue to feel is looking at my husband during this whole process of losing his mother. I just want to fix it and make it better. And I can't.

There has been so much loss. So much worry. So much anxiety. I sometimes feel like a building has fallen on top of me. BUT, I'm strong. I get out from under the rubble of that building and brush myself off. I look at my legs. You can walk. I start to talk. You can tell people you love them. You have arms that can hug. You can breathe. You have life. Live it. And you have been. Throughout this devastating year, you have continued to keep living and leading with love. I'm proud of you. On March 12th, when you

heard you'd be home for 30 days due to a weird virus, don't lie.... you were relieved. Girl, you could barely walk. You couldn't take a deep breath because your ribs hurt so bad. You had no energy to play with Hudson. You couldn't focus. You were beyond burnt out. You walked through that door, snatched your son up and said "I'm yours for a month!" And wasn't it fun for a few days?! Until you realized you had a hard time breathing. You were one of the lucky ones, though. You recovered. Those first few months were some of the best times spent at home. The hikes, all the cooking, all the movies, all the bedtimes. It was heaven. Then the 2nd extension of the shutdown happened. You crumbled. You didn't stop crying for 3 days.

It really hit you that you can't live without this. You need to perform. It's a part of your lifeline. But what did you do? You picked yourself up. You looked out at your beautiful life you have in front of you and you continued to live it. You are living in the most present, focused way. It's a beautiful life. If we've been taught anything this year, it's that life is precious and it can be taken from us in a second. So take advantage of the tiniest moments. Find that little spark of joy everyday, grab it and use it to help reignite that little ember inside you. You know the lights will be bright again, and when they are—you will be a Supernova.

Lead With Love,
Robyn
@RobynHurder

Dear Laura,

When the lights are bright again, I want you to know how proud I am of you. You made it through a year without the thing that lights you up. You searched and found other, smaller, different things to illuminate you in new ways. The feelings of joy and excitement that were usually created from receiving a final callback, from dancing in a room full of sweaty friends, from booking a dream gig....those feelings were found in new places....from a beautiful walk with your family and pup, from a meaningful conversation with friends over Zoom, from your new nightly tradition of watching *Ozark* with your parents, from seeing friends continuing to move forward and inspire, and secretly, from the little glimmer of hope deep down that we would all be back together one day, sharing the ultimate soul illuminator. There were many hard days too... days of numbing just how difficult this was and what it meant for you and the community that you love so much. And that's okay. When you have worked every moment of every day with your entire being to reach a certain point and it is pulled away from you in seconds, gosh darn it how could it not be hard? But you made it. And when the lights are bright again, I promise you will never take one moment of this life for granted. We are lucky, being artists. In my opinion, we have the most special job in the world. We get to share joy with others, to put our whole hearts into our work every night, we get to keep learning and growing and training and struggling and feeling and sharing our gift. Being an artist is special and you did not lose that in this time. You kept your community and even created a stronger community, teaching ballet multiple times a week to many students and professionals of all ages. You created passion projects with friends and connected with new artists along the way. And this kept you going. **Because you are an artist from the deepest place inside you and nothing can take that away.** This year has proved that. And I am proud of you. As the lights slowly return, I want you to remember the balance you have found. You can work hard and still give yourself time to rest. You can still make time for those you love and take care of your heart and you hard working body. You can learn and grow and remember to see things from a broader perspective. And having the time to realize these things was a gift. A gift in a hard year. The other gifts? Precious time with your family, time to educate yourself on important happenings in our world, time to learn and unlearn, time to connect with old friends, and time with the lights dimmed so you can realize just how lucky you are when they are bright again. Our world will never be the same, on a broad level, and in our own community. We have seen and learned too much to go back to the old. So let's welcome the new with open arms. Here's to you and the many artists who made it through this year. I am proud of you.

> We are lucky, being artists. In my opinion we have the most special job in the world. We get to share joy with others....

YUZZZ and love,
Laura
@yuzzz12
Originally from Kansas City, MO

Dear Kristen,

When the lights are bright again, you'll be there. The last year nearly got the best of you, but you didn't let it. It would be easy to focus on all you have lost – your beloved AEA job of 13 years, the regional theatres you loved to work for, your life savings and so much more.

But let's focus on what you gained.

- You gained more knowledge in the past year than some do in a lifetime.

- You received extra time to heal from the injury you were JUST coming back to work from the day everything shut down.

- You gained independence and safety when your mentally/emotionally abusive relationship ended.

- You found ways to pay for your house and all the bills you were left with.

- You co-founded a cookie company with a fellow actor friend during the shut-down to lift the spirits of your community.

- You found some work in your field even though it was all but gone.

- You learned a slew of new skills (stilt walking!).

- You cultivated the most beautiful friendship with your ex-husband and work as his assistant on his dance photo shoots.

- You sought out a counselor to work through- not around- all the hardships and heartbreaks you faced.

- You did it on your own, in the midst of a pandemic, though you were hardly alone. You had the most incredible support system to help you along the way, and you learned to let them help.

- You didn't need a pandemic to remind you of how much you love the stage. Every single day a memory would pop into your head, bringing tears to your eyes and a sting to your heart. You just wanted to know it would come back someday, and you would have the opportunity to stand on a stage again.

It would have been so easy to just give up. To give in to those really dark days. But you didn't.

You kept moving forward.

When you get onstage again it will be electric. You have a brand-new perspective on life.

When the lights are bright again, YOU WILL BE READY.

I am so proud of you.

> **Every single day a memory would pop into your head, bringing tears to your eyes and a sting to your heart**

Love,
Kristen
@kristensheola
Originally from Long Valley, NJ

JOY

Dear Mel,

When the lights are bright again, you're gonna cry.

Because, let's face it, you're a faucet when you feel. A leaky sensitive spout.

Too happy, too sad, too hungry – water works. Like it or not, you are a feeler, my dear, and that is a beautiful (sometimes inconvenient) thing.

You have been crying this year for all the auditions that didn't happen, for all your friends who didn't make their Broadway debuts, for the weeks spent in your tiny apartment in Washington Heights, for all the headshots you had printed and couldn't use, for the lack of opportunity for your craft that you so passionately adore.

You have been crying over the boy who couldn't love you enough to stay, for your mom's diagnosis that happened in the Fall, for missing your best friend's wedding and having to watch it at a kitchen table (alone) drunk off a bottle of champagne.

There have already been so many tears of grief, loss and despondence this year from you.

(I can't imagine how many tears the Earth has held this year – the tears of the millions who have lost loved ones to this virus, who have lost jobs, who have lost purpose, who have lost their drive, their sense of self…)

But –

When the lights are bright again you're gonna cry tears of relief that your community is back, that **a renaissance is among us**, that soon you will be sitting in those velvet chairs while listening to an overture that will make your heart swell so big you think it will burst.

You're gonna cry when your mom is able to come and see you in your next show (because there will be a next show), when you get to show off your new love, when you get to hold and kiss friends who you have only seen in 2-D the last year.

When the lights are bright again you're gonna cry – but these will be sparkly happy tears pouring out of a golden grateful faucet.

Get those tissues ready babe, it's coming.

I'm proud of you,
Mel
@melweyn
Originally from Alpharetta, GA

> Like it or not, you are a feeler my dear and that is a beautiful (sometimes inconvenient) thing.

Dear Rachel,

When the lights are bright again, it might be quiet at first. It might be somber. There might be safety protocols, or smaller companies, or intimate audiences. **Revel in the quiet.** Enjoy the gentle hum of the orchestra tune-up, the moment of pure stillness before the first downbeat and audience applause, and the liminal space where art and reality collide.

I know you're hurt and upset, enough that it took you months to even touch a wig again after everything shut down. Hurt that our government has done NOTHING to support people and businesses are forced to stay open. You don't blame them, but it doesn't make it hurt any less. What you want people to understand most is how long and hard you fought for your career, and how having it all ripped from you in a single weekend is making you question all the missed birthdays, holiday celebrations, get togethers, and coming home to a husband who is already asleep 6 nights a week.

You are vowing right here and now to never again be plagued with the self doubt and imposter syndrome that made you feel like you didn't deserve your own success, because you didn't realize just how much you belonged somewhere until it was taken from you. Be focused, be present, and FLY HIGH. Let this be a lesson to never take your industry for granted.

You also found unexpected joy in being at home so much! You grew a beautiful garden over the summer, took better care of yourself physically, cooked more meals, and protested injustices you aren't even going to get into in this letter because it's a whole other conversation. Most of all, you learned that the cult of busyness is overrated and it's OK to not constantly be GOING. When the lights are bright again, and you can go back to work, I am begging you to share that joy.

Please don't let your own light that you've cultivated to keep burning during the darkness of the past year slink back into the shadows.

All my (self) love,
Rachel
@rachelmakesartandwigs
Originally from Waukegan, IL

> Revel
> in the
> quiet.

SHEREEN PIMENTEL
Originally from
Teaneck, NJ

Dear Shereen,

When the lights are bright again remember rainbows always come after a storm. This time gave you the opportunity to look inward and find yourself outside of what you do. I think it's so easy for artists to define themselves by this label – "Hi my name is {insert name} and I am a {insert talent}." What happens when all of that stops? That doesn't mean you're no longer an artist, but now you think about what else is out there in the world. What hobbies you may like and never picked up, places you've never been, things you want to work on but never had time for. I struggled with who I was outside of being a performer. But now after 2 years of picking up as many hobbies as I could, getting a puppy and finding other things that I'm interested in; I feel strength in who I am. I can't wait for it all to start again and when it starts I'll bring all of these things with me because I'm more than just a performer. I'm a multi-faceted human. I leave you with these lyrics I wrote

**"Live in the moment
Remember the day
Before it's all gone and
you've gone away"**

The only limit you have is the one you set for yourself.

With love,
Shereen
@shereenpimentel

> ...I'm more than just a performer. I'm a multi-faceted human.

Dear Robin,

When the lights are bright again you will look back on this time and marvel at the strength, resiliency and hope that you shared with your beloved fellow theater community... and the world. I write this at the year mark of you packing your last bags from New York City and making that blind faith move back home to start a job that would soon end in the shocking face of the global pandemic. That feeling of helplessness as we all watched, prayed and loved on our family and friends from afar still stings. I am proud that you held your head higher than your anxieties and faced what stood in your way for so long... you surrendered your old worries and stood with the rest of the world in fear and hope from your living room. **You've had a humbling dose of perspective.** You let go of the ideas of who you thought you were called to be and do in this life and told yourself it's ok... if I have failed it's ok... if I've let myself and others down it's ok... and if I want to start over again right here and now that's ok. You forgave yourself for all the times fear stood in your way of going after your ambitions with full unstoppable force like not going to that audition when you had the chance when the lights were indeed bright... well when the lights are bright again you will have realized how precious life is and to be here and healthy with dreams in my heart and a fire in my soul is a gift. You will embrace your fellow dream makers and soak up the ever so precious once in a lifetime moments that theater emulates. And what a privilege and honor it will be to no longer stand in your own way as you pursue alongside your courageous colleagues and friends the love of creating and sharing. You have realized your identity and worth is not made from your achievements... those come and go. **A well rounded, balanced, and truly happy joyous life is loving where you are in the very moment you are in it...** And those moments each accumulate into the intricate, layered, teary, laughter filled, ever changing, heart broken, giddy, grateful canvas that is your unfinished journey. I am proud of your unfinished journey. Get to work, be happy where you are and don't rush your time.

Robin Elizabeth
@robin.aren
Originally from Chicago, IL

> ...dream those dreams you've always dreamt.

Dear Gian,

When the lights are bright again you'll get a chance. To be who you were meant to be. To do what you were meant to do. To feel what you were meant to feel. To dream those dreams you've always dreamt. To hold your head up high. To collaborate. To hug someone. To sing out loud. To dance in the streets. To smile. To shine. To shine brighter. To shine brighter than those lights. To be you. One hundred percent you.

Stay strong. Stay bright. Stay you.
Gian
@gi_raffaele
Oringally from North Smithfield, RI

> A well rounded, balanced, and truly happy joyous life is loving where you are in the very moment you are in...

Dear Josh

> **...his grin was so big even his mask couldn't hide it.**

Dear Ty,

When the lights are bright again, don't hesitate. Be you, all of you, full out, no marking bitch! You are officially done being who you think people want you to be. You have my permission to exist in your fullness (they'll adjust). Continue to trust your instincts and remember I love you. It's ok, I promise.

Always yours,
Ty
@thetybrand
Originally from Charlotte, NC

> **I love you. It's ok, I promise.**

When the lights are bright again you'll still remember that year. You'll remember having so many hopes and goals and dreams for 2020, only to find yourself frantically packing a rental car on March 16th to leave NYC and drive to your parent's house. You'll remember those first few weeks. The uncertainty, the fear, the boredom. You'll remember the warm Maryland summer and planting a garden with your mom. You'll remember going through boxes of your old stuff packed away from decades past. You'll remember putting on a one man show streamed for all the world to see from the comforts of your parent's basement. You'll remember nights sitting at the dinner table with Mom and Dad talking about the news or anything but the news, please anything but the news. You'll remember building the treehouse in your backyard for your nephew. Finally, building a treehouse that you'd wanted to build when you were a kid but never did. Taking all of August to build. You'll remember the joy on your nephew's face when he finally came up to your parent's house to see it; **his grin was so big that even his mask couldn't hide it.** You'll remember the sadness you felt at times, the loneliness and isolation. You'll remember the people you loved that you reached out to for support and the ones you supported. You'll remember the quiet snowy winter nights and the warm, summer afternoon bike rides. You'll remember the first time you got to step back on stage in NY, performing in a small play about civil rights. No audience of course, just a few cameras recording the action. You'll remember packing the car again, giving Mom and Dad a hug and saying I love you. You'll remember seeing the NYC skyline again, the one that you'd left in such a hurry one year ago. You'll remember the lives lost. You'll remember the talented people who all had a million different experiences and stories, who all went their own ways only to return, because the show must go on eventually...when the lights are bright again.

Josh
@joshdnyc
Originally from Ellicott City, MD

> **Share your light as much as you can, even if others try to dim it.**

Dear Cody,

When the lights are bright again, you might be emotional. You might be flooded with feelings of relief and joy and anxiety and nerves and hope and loss and your love for theatre and so much more. Whatever happens, I urge you to take this moment for yourself.

Stand there.

Soak it in.

Breathe.

And just be.

Take this moment and let it wash over you. Breathe in the light and breathe out any negative energy that may linger. Use this as fuel to re-enter a territory that is familiar and, at the same time, very new. Embrace this new territory and infuse it with new energy – energy that allows space for others to feel comfortable and welcomed, energy that uplifts and is vibrant, joyful and full of love.

The road to the lights being bright again has been a long one, and you owe it to yourself to take this moment in and cherish every minute of it. Remember the lessons that this last year has taught you. Remember to stay committed to your mission of making space for others. And remember to stand in your truth and that your purpose is greater than anyone's permission.

Continue to operate from a place of joy and love. Walk into every rehearsal room, every stage door, every office, and every space with your Black Joy – live unapologetically and be true to your essence. Share your light as much as you can, even if others try to dim it.

For when the lights are bright again, you may be flooded with so many emotions, but enjoy your ability to stand in the light and in your gratitude. This moment must not be rushed. Walk in your power, because just like Dolly Levi…"you are back where you belong," baby!

With endless love,
Cody Renard Richard
@codyrenard

CODY RENARD RICHARD
Originally from
Houston, TX

Dear Eloise,

When the lights are bright again, and they will be bright again, everything will be different. Because you are different.

This year has changed everyone, this year has changed the world, and this year has changed you. This year has opened up the deepest parts of yourself. The parts of yourself that are usually covered by the makeup, the bright lights, the applause, and the stories that take you away.

At first the shutdown felt like a punishment. Everything you've worked so hard for was taken away in an instant. The only thing that gave you worth and helped you feel alive was gone. Everyone around you seamlessly switched to this "virtual world," and all you wanted to do was scream and shout about how it was not the same. The passions that used to light you up and motivate you to get up each morning, no longer did. The lights on the stage and the world were shut off, and you had to meet yourself and ask;

In a world where theatre doesn't exist, who are you and what do you love?

These were the questions that you started to ask yourself. This was the way you started to dip your toes into new adventures, new challenges, and new passions.
Started to dream
and soften
and listen
and love
And let go
And heal
You started to illuminate the daily doings and accept the new mystery that was unfolding right in front of you…
Your life.

Eloise, nothing is for certain. Every breath is a step on the journey that is your life. Fill it with a little bit of everything and always remember to surround yourself with those who fill up your heart, not take away. Accept the mystery of it all unfolding and make it sacred.

Believe in the curiosity, the joy, and the heart that lies within you.

2020 was the year you realized the whole world is a stage!!!

> *Live in it sweet girl,*
> *Xx*
> **Me**
> @eloisekropp
> Originally from Edmond, OK

> **"** …nothing is for certain. Every breath is a step on the journey that is your life. **"**

Dear Johnny,

When the lights are bright again, jump for joy. Shout from the rooftops how fortunate you are to be one of the lucky ones who made it back. When the lights are bright again, make being kind your job. **Lift others up and bring more people into the light.** Never forget the long road behind you and the long road ahead.

Oh and hug your stage management team and never let them go.

Love,
Johnny
@johnny_milani
Originally from Jacksonville, FL

Dear Chelsey,

When the lights are bright again you will remember what it's like to feel the rush of joy. You will remember why all these years you worked so hard. You will remember why so many mornings you woke up at 4 am and hustled. You will remember why you pounded the pavement. You will remember why you worked so many ridiculous jobs to make this life happen. You will remember why you love what you do. You will remember what it feels like to hear the roar of an audience. You will remember how it feels to get that rush before the curtain opens. You will remember why you were put on this Earth. You will remember how to love again. When the lights are bright again, you will remember why you are here.

All my love,
Chelsey
@chelseylapix
Originally from New York, NY

> "...hug your stage management team and never let them go."

> "You chose this career path because you wanted to bring people joy through art."

Dear Andrew,

When the lights are bright again, every ounce of fear or doubt that you have felt this past year will have all been worth it. You will take your first entrance as a completely different person than when you took your last exit. Cherish every moment. You chose this career path because you wanted to bring people joy through art. People need that now more than ever. You've been given this time to reenergize. You're getting ready to hear "places" for what is about to be the most exhilarating, enlightening, and groundbreaking era of art and theatre this world has seen. It's up to us to help heal, uplift, and change, so go eat some chicken nuggets and get ready to sing, kid. You love what you do and you can't see yourself doing anything else, so quit doubting yourself.

Stay curious, stay positive, stay hopeful,
Andrew
@andrewposton96
Originally from Pamplico, SC

Dear Will,

as in "we WILL",

When the lights are bright again, be happy that you made the decisions you made. To work in this incredible theater industry, and to shift to another incredible industry during this weird time. Be fulfilled in your transition from artistic creator to supporter, from performer to audience member. **Feel joy for those on stage, and know that heartbreak is part of it too.** Be proud of your choices. To pursue this crazy life, to take chances, and to continue doing it in so many ways. Your name exudes optimism. Reflect that as we move into the future.

I love you.
Will, as in "we WILL"
Originally from Cary, NC

Dear MC,

When the lights are bright again…

After the "live-with-your-parents-in-the-midwest-for-six-months" part of quarantine ended, I returned to my beloved New York. With tears streaming down my face in the back of a yellow cab, I vowed to never stay away that long again.

It felt so soul-nourishing to be back in my own apartment and among my community. New York's gorgeous fall weather was beginning to flirt, numbers were down, and in true NYC fashion, it seemed the city had adapted to the times with flying colors.

And then in nearly the same breath, the magic faded and I really realized that my life in New York was no longer my life in New York. I had come home to a familiar place with a very unfamiliar direction and purpose. I didn't know this New York. I didn't know how to relate to the city without theatre. My body had served up a health puzzle six months prior, nearly in sync with the shutdown, which made singing incredibly frustrating. Without my instrument and my industry, I was completely lost.

So I took myself to the Ambassador to say hello, and I cried on the street. It felt so good to be in its presence again and honor the sacred ground that it is for me. It is one of the most important places I'd go to fill up and experience my artist self. And it was my home away from home.

The next month, I began working a new survival job on west 39th street, and I frequently took a detour to say my hello to the theatre. Each day to and from work, I also started passing the Nederlander, which is where I made my Broadway debut. Despite their dormancy, I couldn't stay away from my old haunts. I desperately needed to drink in their memories and feel connected to my New York.

One day, I felt especially blue, so I took my ten block walk to say hello. In a flurry of instinct, I ripped this tiny little sticker of a keyboard off of the back of my AirPod case and stuck it to the the stage door of the Ambassador, right next to the *Mean Girls* ad.

In retrospect, I guess I had a guttural need to leave a tangible piece of me there until I have the incredible honor of gracing its stage again. What a joyous and meaningful day that will be. Until then, when the lights are finally bright again, I'll just keep saying hi – to make sure I'm still a part of it all.

Love,
MC
@murrclurr
Originally from Columbus, IN

> **With tears streaming down my face in the back of a yellow cab, I vowed to never stay away that long again.**

Dear Lisa,

When the lights are bright again all around the world. WOW what a sight it will be!

Those that know me, know that I don't believe in stress. Well, 2020 shook and tested that belief to my core. I knew from the time I was 10 years old that theater would be my life's journey.

Therefore no one nor nothing can or will steal "my joy."

The following quotes, statements, phrases and prayers helped and continue to help me through this separateness caused by both the pandemic and the "awakening."

- When quick judgments are made, mistakes are bound to happen. Take your time to learn and really see someone's character.

- Careful not to become the oppressor.

- *We are more alike, my friends, than we are unalike.* – Maya Angelou

- *No one is born hating another person because of the color of their skin, or their background, or their religion. People must learn to hate, and if they can learn to hate, they can be taught to love, for love comes more naturally to the human heart than its opposite.* – Nelson Mandela

- The loudest voice doesn't determine the direction to go.

- In the midst of chaos, breathe. There is a steadiness inside you.

- You must be the change you wish to see in the world.

- Every day is a second chance.

- The desire to reach hearts is wise and most possible.

- Be KIND. Be a rainbow in someone's cloud.

Love, Compassion, Empathy
Lisa Dawn
@lisadawncave

> " The loudest voice doesn't determine the direction to go. "

Dear Drew,

When the lights are bright again, remember to keep those showtunes on blast.

It wasn't until Broadway went dark that you even thought to turn the volume back up. Remember how Little Drew once bathed himself in cast recordings? **Those albums fueled your self-confidence and kept you dancing through adolescence.** You screamed *West Side* in the bedroom and blared "Ragtime" in the classroom during your report on the Industrial Revolution. And, like a proper homosexual, "No Day But Today" was proudly stamped beneath your senior yearbook photo: you were so damn cool and cultured.

Then at eighteen, you moved to New York and stumbled ego-first into the hustle and grind of auditions. Somewhere between rejections and insecurities, you turned the showtunes way down: *A Chorus Line* doesn't sparkle the same way when you don't book the national tour.

But when Broadway suddenly went dark in midtown last March, the curtain went up in your central Harlem apartment. Dancing through the kitchen, tapping in the living room, singing in the shower, chopping vegetables to Bernadette: **Little Drew and his love for showtunes came back to visit this year, and what a gift to remember the pure magic that swirls between every overture and finale.** Those scores that planted the seed of a dream decades ago came back in full bloom during quarantine. Thank God.

> ## You are more than a callback.

Although the metaphorical carpet of your career has been ripped out from underneath you this last year, don't forget what 365-days of bedroom show tune jams have taught you. You are more than a callback. You are more than falling out of a single pirouette in front of Tony winners. You are more than your forty-five-degree battement. You've spent a decade desperately wishing you could be every other Broadway muscle chorus boy but yourself, and it took a global pandemic to teach you that there is nobody else in the world for you to be but Drew.

So, when the mundanities of the hustle come rushing back, remember how much of a light you already are. Do your best to compartmentalize the "show" from "the biz" and know that the weight of your spirit is not determined by an 8 x 10 frame. You are enough, you always have been. And most importantly, keep those showtunes on blast.

Love,
Inner Child Drew
@drewkingNYC
Originally from Sterling, MA

Dear Katie,

When the lights are bright again, you will refind the inner glow which went into hiding the day the world and every theater shut down. You will pull open the heavy stage door again and sign your name on the call board before getting appropriately caffeinated. You will feel overwhelming emotion at the stage manager's voice calling "Places, please." and "Five minutes to the top of Act Two." You will play your heart out in the sweeping wave of the overture's opening flourish. (And your bow will be freshly rehaired so those strings will SING!) You will share intermission water cooler chats and between-show meals with colleagues who have become friends. You will play sound checks in wildly different acoustics, grind through the exhaustion of tech week and share the collective giddy excitement of opening night. You will catch the conductor's eye before downbeat and smile, knowing the unspoken shared thought is "See you on the other side!!" **You will allow yourself to feel profound joy again** in telling a story through the magic of music, theatre and dance. You will probably cry a lot. You will also laugh deeply, smile with your whole heart and be overwhelmed with joy, relief and gratitude. You will never again doubt your passion for this beautiful art form, because it is only when our greatest loves in life are taken away that we truly realize how much they mean to us. But until that unfathomably special day arrives, Katie... take care of yourself. Take care of your people. Keep practicing! And most importantly, don't ever give up faith in your life's purpose and love. **The world needs music. Few things are more nourishing to the soul than a truly beautiful melody.** And you bet your bottom dollar that New York City needs theatre. We will be back. And we will set the world on fire.

All my love,
Katie
@kveebee
Originally from New York, NY

> ## We will be back. And we will set the world on fire.

ESSENTIAL

Dear Tiny Dancer,

When the lights are bright again...the words "what I did for love" will never be the same.

When the lights are bright again...you'll dance. You'll dance like no one is watching and like everyone is watching because the joy you feel when you dance deserves to be felt and seen.

When the lights are bright again...you'll sing. You'll sing not like a dancer who is self-conscious of her range but like a woman who is loud and proud of her voice and will never be silenced again.

When the lights are bright again...you'll give yourself grace. Grace because you survived. Survived trauma and heartbreak and came out stronger. **A new you. More resilient. Badass.**

When the lights are bright again...you'll still miss those we lost. Every day. But you'll look at life differently. Every breath is a reminder of how your body is still carrying you. Keep going.

When the lights are bright again...you'll remember all you sacrificed to keep your family safe. Every dance class in your bedroom, every voice lesson in the garage was worth it. Saying goodbye to friends, jobs, your livelihood for over a year was worth it. Worth it because you never forgot who you are. Never forgot what matters most. Theatre will be back and you'll be alive when it does.

When the lights are bright again...you'll love. The kind of can't eat, can't sleep, over the moon type of love. Love that doesn't judge. Love that coexists with our perfect imperfections.

When the lights are bright again...you'll take your bow under those bright lights with pride knowing how hard you worked to get there. You kept going even though some days the anxiety and depression felt like it was too much to bare. You're a fighter.

When the lights are bright again...you'll laugh. A laugh that isn't coupled with guilt.

When the lights are bright again...you'll be enough. Enough for you and enough for them.

When the lights are bright again...you'll be bright again too.

I am so proud of you.

Keep chasing those dreams!
Tiny Dancer <3
@angie.colonna
Originally from Palm City, FL

Dear Jennifer,

When the lights are bright again

So your soul will be

Bright with the vibrance of the *Hamilton* family.

Rather daunting, sitting before a blank page

With the intention of pouring out

About a year without the stage.

Your forever dream had just come true

And when the lights are bright again

You will feel Broadway's lights, too.

I know it feels

It's been forever, and more

But it will feel like no time has passed

When you open that stage door.

Holding onto hope,
Jennifer
@SpongeJenniferBob
Originally from Marietta, GA

> ## Your forever dream had just come true.

> ## We have to hold on to the dream. And I will. We need to.

Dear Elizabeth,

When the lights are bright again, you may feel so many overwhelming things at once. You will feel overwhelmed at first, because you know you will be jealous of certain people. Then you will feel yourself relax. You have thought of this for many years, that jealousy is a waste of time. You are truly on your own path, which is why you have been on the journey you have been on the last few years. Everyone is on their own path, and when the lights are bright again, you will find a way to get your dream to come true. To help people. To lift people up. To support those who truly need it. To celebrate people. As they sing in *Man of La Mancha—*" This is my quest, to follow that star

No matter how hopeless, no matter how far." We have to hold on to the dream. And I will. We need to.

When the lights are bright again, we will be able to reach those dreams. No matter what the road map looks like.

Elizabeth
@Emaxman1
Originally from New York, NY

Dear Christian,

When the lights are bright again, your light will shine even brighter. No one could've imagined the traumatic roller coaster 2020 would be. Beyond the painful moments that seemed never-ending, there was light at the end of the tunnel. I'm grateful that every moment was a learning lesson. What I know for sure is that I needed this time to be still and realign myself. I've refocused my artistic purpose. I now know where I need to be of service. I've always strove to illuminate black excellence in everything I was apart of within the theater. Now it is time to expand, develop, and create everything I felt wasn't there for people like me. The lights will never be the same again. More importantly I believe our inner lights have shifted and sharpened. We must be rid of the old white standards that have imprisoned diverse voices within our industry and collectively lean into a world where everyone has a seat at the table. Our duty has always been to reflect the community. I hope when you look in the mirror that reflection is a new warrior of change. I plan on fearlessly building the world I want to live in. No limits, no filter, all love and light. I pray the same for anyone reading this. The change is the light. We are the change. We are the light. I am the light. I am the change.

Christian
@christiandante

CHRISTIAN DANTE WHITE
Originally from
South Bend, IN

"The lights will never be the same again. More importantly I believe our inner lights have shifted and sharpened."

Querida Reyna,

When the lights are bright again/Cuando las luces vuelven a brillar…

En una inesperada encrucijada de la vida, nos encontramos enclaustrados en una obscuridad. Por más de un año, hemos vivido una vida sin luz. El primer día ninguno de nosotros pensaba que se iba a convertir en una semana, un mes, un año. ¿Es posible regresar a la vida que teníamos antes?

Recuerda que nuestros padres sacrificaron tanto para nosotros. Nuestros padres pusieron todo en riesgo no más para poder lograr ese "sueño americano." ¿Ahora vamos a llorar porque nos apagaron las luces? ¿Amigos, que les pasa? Si nos apagaron las luces- Pues órale, enciéndalas.

No vayan a pensar que yo no sufrí. Yo si sufrí, y GACHO. Yo ni puedo empezar a escribir lo GACHO que he sentido. Amigos, les confieso que yo no crecí con una abuela en casa. La única abuela que yo he conocido es ABUELA CLAUDIA. Abuela Claudia nos dio un consejo a todos: PACIENCIA Y FÉ. Abuela Claudia nos recuerda que nosotros somos de tierra, sangre, y gente bendita. Abuela Claudia nos recuerda que TENEMOS que "ALZAR LA BANDERA." Así que regreso a mi pregunta, es posible regresar a la vida que teníamos antes? NO.

Nos han sofocado. Nos han matado en nuestras propias casas. Nos han quitado nuestra identidad. Nos han robado nuestras historias.

Mi gente, CUANDO LAS LUCES VUELVEN A BRILLAR, recuerda lo tanto que le rogaste a Dios por este momento. Recuerda que tú eres más de lo que tus antepasados se podrían imaginar. Más que nada, con el inglés mas matado que nada, con el nopal en la frente, recuerda lo que el maestro Emilio Estefan dijo, "THIS IS WHAT AN AMERICAN LOOKS LIKE."

Atte:
Reyna de Jesús, Stillness of July
@reynadjesus
Originally from Torreón, Coahuila, México

> "THIS IS WHAT AN AMERICAN LOOKS LIKE."

Dear Charlene,

When the lights are bright again, you will look back and know that you did exactly what you were supposed to do and that you are exactly where you are supposed to be. You worked hard to keep your family safe and happy. You gave them joyful memories during a time that crushed your soul. You said goodbye to an apartment of 18 years that you moved into fresh off of the road and newly in love and you left as a wife and a mother. You learned how to use Zoom for virtual holiday gatherings with your family, Broadway show reunions, educational seminars, meetings, and guest appearances in virtual high school and college classrooms across the country.

When the lights are bright again, you will hold your breath in anticipation of the downbeat and cry tears of joy to see something you love so very much come to life again. You will be wiser, kinder, and you will have more compassion for your entire community.

When the lights are bright again, you will witness a community that has recognized its shortcomings and will come forward with a unified voice of inclusivity and acceptance.

When the lights are bright again, you will watch as the rest of the world comes to realize what you've known all along – live theatre is life-giving, soul nurturing and most of all, essential.

For now, theater's rebirth feels impossible, but take comfort in knowing that each day that passes is one day closer to the day when the lights are bright again.

Be safe, be well and be kind,
CS
@cspeyerer
Originally from Plano, TX

Dear Megan,

When the lights are bright again life won't look much different for you than it does now, but your perspective will. You will still be jobless and focusing on health and family. That sense of relief you felt during the Pandemic will end. However, the space and strength you gained will reshape your relationship with the Business. Your magical gifts will not always be the right fit for the job, but now you can stand in your power and have nothing to prove. You are enough without the job and capable of more than most give you credit for. When the day comes that you share a Broadway stage with the other unicorns of the world, you will breathe in every second and know how truly lucky you are to be a part of this community. Until then, you have a full and beautiful life that allows you continuous growth and so much love.

XOXO,
Megan
@megansikora
Originally from Pittsburgh, PA

Hey KB,

When the lights are bright again, promise me three things.

1. Continue speaking from the authentic voice you have found during this time of heartache. Never try to emulate other people, for their journey is theirs and your journey is yours.

2. Never put the weight of your worth in the praise others offer again. Put the weight of your worth in how you make others feel, the intentions of your heart, and the courage of your soul.

3. Stop trying to impress a room full of white men. Is their opinion or their judgement usually correct anyways? Didn't think so.

If you're able to hold true to these three things when the lights are bright again, I'd say that you are pretty much nailing it.

Xoxo,
Kat
@kat_brunner
Originally from Hatboro, PA

CHERIE B. TAY
Originally from
Houston, TX/ Singapore

Dear Cherie,

When the lights are bright again, remember the perseverance and togetherness that got us through.

From lifting others up in solidarity, to finding growth and change within yourself.

Keep exploring your own dreams that "you never had time for."

Keep on learning how to use your voice to stand up for yourself and others.

Take a deep breath once in a while and remind yourself that you're going to be okay.

When the lights are bright again, cherish it, honor it, and make it a better, safer space for all.

Cherie
@cheriebtay

"...remember the perseverance and togetherness that got us through."

Dear Marc,

When the lights are bright again, we'll be essential again, too. We shut down our stages, our tours, our lives, to help keep other people safe. We didn't ask questions, we followed the rules, we masked up, we Zoomed, we waited patiently, longingly to be back to work and doing what we do. While those on the front lines gave the most urgent care, we will help them heal the wounds. We will bring the joy back, bring the laughs, bring the tears. What we do may not have been essential to saving lives, but it will always be a vital part of being alive.

Until then,
Marc
@marcviscardi
Originally from Rochester, NY

> " When the lights are bright again, we'll be essential again, too. We shut down our stages, our tours, our lives, to help keep other people safe. "

Dear James,

When The Lights Are Bright Again: Theater was knocked to the canvas in 2020 as were arena shows and other live events. My brothers and sisters are suffering. We hear about essential services all the time and yes food and health care top the list. But when it's time for the curtain to rise and the lights come up we will all have a newfound and profound appreciation for another essential service: Arts and Entertainment. We need this emotional nourishment as surely as we need food and shelter and good health. And our stagehands and crafts people will know this to be true by the appreciative and deafening applause and shouts from their audiences as the bright lights shine once again. We're almost there.

James
Originally from Sparta, NJ

Dear Angela,

When the lights are bright again you will still be meant for this. There is a reason God or the universe or whoever gave you this passion. I know you feel lost and question every day whether you were meant for this, but you are. There is no doubt. You've been gifted the drive to make your dreams happen. So, slow down, enjoy where you are, and hold onto what is coming. Because it's coming.

Holding onto hope,
Angela
@ang_larose1
Originally from Sugarloaf, PA

Dear Mitchell Pressel,

When the lights are bright again, you will continue working.

It was a huge blow to you when the world shut down. It's pretty hard to believe that Broadway has been shut down for more than a year now. You kept seeing these Instagram stories of people ridiculing and mocking Covid-19, and going directly against CDC guidelines for their own self-benefit. It continued to make you increasingly more angry and upset when you saw this same trend, however, with a past teacher of the arts, a favorite director or choreographer, or someone who you loved and respected.

The year before Covid, you were pushing all in. You were doing rigorous training from Performers Theater Workshop in Maplewood, The Paper Mill Playhouse Summer Conservatory, (which is nationally known), and three musicals at a time. You were doing a show in New York, at a drag bar called Don't Tell Mama. Six or seven agents and managers were invited to come see the show. You did four shows in two days. After the final two show day, you received an email saying there was interest. Three separate agents wanted to sign you. Then Covid happened. You were stuck in an endless loop of, "Is it going to happen? No. How about now? No." Self tape audition after self tape, mp3 after mp3. You had to find a way to continue your artistry during a time where you couldn't go outside without putting a fucking cloth on your face.

A year later and you're doing better than you ever have. You have just finished filming *You're a Good Man, Charlie Brown*, and you're currently doing *Singin' in the Rain*. You receive a few auditions a week from your agent over at Stewart, and you're loving it. You strive to be Evan Hansen every day. **You're simply learning, working, and waiting for the right opportunities.**

Love,
Mitchell
@heymitchellpressel
Originally from Maplewood, NJ

Dearest Lauren,

When the lights are bright again, I hope you will remember you are not defined by them. There is no one who can take away your voice, even in the dark. Remember the day you were asked the ordinarily normal question of what you did for work, and from some faraway place of doubt and fear, you answered "I used to be a singer." Remember the tears that followed, each one a release of the grief you've been holding, a reflection of your true love for the art form, a reminder of the arduous years of work. **In breaking your own heart with that single sentence, it showed you the way forward, a map to your undeniable belonging in this community.** The only difficulty is in the waiting. I hope you show up time and time again, willing to bet on yourself, your ability, and your hard work. The electric sense of possibility. The nerve of all that hope. They live in the audacity to try just one more time. Turn that truth over and over. Believe those days are coming, sooner than you know. Imagine this time for what it is, standing in the wings, hearing the overture, enveloped in delicious anticipation for what's to come. I hope you revel in how glorious it will be when we all might be able to recognize ourselves, stepping out of the dark, and into those lights again.

That is what I wish for you. I am holding your hands, the space for your dreams, and a watchful eye on your rightful place downstage. Always.

Coraggio, my dear, and all my love,
Lauren
@lyokabaskas
Originally from Cape Elizabeth, ME

> " There is no one who can take away your voice, even in the dark. "

> ## "You stayed on the path, you weathered the storm, you held your friend's hands..."

Dear Katie,

When the lights are bright again, you will know that this time of reflection helped you to understand just how much you love costume design. How much you love the theatre. It isn't just work, it is a career, a way of life. Next time you read this, I hope that you are smelling the smell of the fabric stores you are shopping in, have sore feet from running around the city all day, laughing with your new friends who are also working on your show, fumbling around in the dark at your tech table to take notes and feeling just as grateful as you feel today knowing that unlike so many you are fortunate enough to pursue your dreams. You have come so far from your high school theatre competition days, to your intern and PA days, to where you are now. **I hope you know how lucky you are that you were brave and strong enough to keep on this path, no matter how uncertain.** I hope you always remember what it was like to walk down an empty Broadway with the lights dark, and never to complain again about the hoards of people lining the streets. I hope you always remember the tears and aching for the next time you would step into a theatre, for that was the exact moment you knew just how much it meant to you. I hope you always remember to continue to support those in your community who have watched after you and you after them during this emotional time because you were in it together. May you always know that your path as a designer was full of ups and downs, but you did it. You stayed on the path, you weathered the storm, you held your friends' hands who also work in the industry, and you persevered. Future Katie, I am so proud. I hope you are working on the Broadway show of your dreams.

Holding onto hope and love,
Katie
Originally from Miami, FL

Dear Sis,

Hey Queen, you do know that you're that girl right? You are constantly raising the bar for us all and doing it flawlessly. For quite some time you have been wearing many hats as a black women in this world does, but through all that giving very recently you have been focusing on the most important hat of all... you! Always keep that hat on! You can't pour from an empty glass baby girl.

You are a vessel.
A vessel for representation.
A vessel for hope.
A vessel for remembrance.
And most importantly a vessel for the future.
We need you here!
Always remember the power that lies inside you. It was adorned on you for a reason. Never forget that.

Continue to change the idea and understanding of creativity. Show them how to breed innovation. Always breed art that is derived from the heart. Continue to give voice to those who are being spoken over. Tell your story!

Like much of my life, this year has been a continuous fight. Divest. You don't have to give your all to these institutions! They don't deserve that from you. Pour into your creativity and dreams. You are the change we wish to see!

Remember autonomy is your greatest asset! The agency over your space and your dreams and your time. It is precious. It is valid. Hold tight to that.

In this industry we are taught to bow down to the powers that be. No. You are the power. Just be!

If we start going back into these spaces with gravitas and control, being our full selves, and willing to call out what should and shouldn't stand–that is when real change will occur.

People like you need to be behind those tables.
Telling stories.
Telling our stories.
Showcasing our existence as we exist.

Please hear me when I say this...
You have exactly what you need.
Your dreams will take you where you need to go.
You have everything you need.
You matter.
They want you to succeed.
You matter.
Oh and one more...YOU ARE THEE BADDEST B*TCH!

Your place in the world is ever so vital for our success and we are so blessed to have you.

Sis
@ucancallmesis

Dear Imperfect Branch,

When the lights are bright again, I hope that you will emerge from this time and always remember how strong you are. I hope that you will carry forth the evidence of all you, the entire theatre community, and the world at large, came through and the courage, strength, compassion, and wisdom it took to make it to this day. None of that disappears. It will always be available to you. The truth is, it always was. I hope that you will remember that your career has given you tools that brought you through this. This is not the first time you have had to find your purpose, your place in this world, when you were not working. This is not the first time you have had to invent your opportunities to be creative when none were available to you. This is not the first time you were told to stop, be still, wait, listen, and hold on to your soul in the quiet. I hope that gratitude, trust, and joy will lead you instead of fear. I hope that you will never forget how Music– that thing you have cherished and loved more than anything– brought you through this time, healing your soul, keeping you in touch with your feelings, getting you outside of your head, encouraging you to raise your eyes to the world around you, and pulling you forward each and every day. I hope that you will continue to be lifted by the things that carried you through: the relationships that were there before, during, and will be there after. They are the through-line of your life. They are the place where you should invest the largest part of your heart. I hope you will never lose that feeling you get, your favorite feeling in the world, when you open the stage door and walk thru it every working day.

Love,
Branch. Imperfectly.
@asintree
Originally from Upland, CA

> " I hope that you will continue to be lifted by the things that carried you through: the relationships that were there before during, and will be there after. "

> ## I have undeniably changed.

Dear Liz who stayed in NYC,

When the lights are bright again...

I grew up in a house with depression and violent behaviors.

In our wicker rocker with headphones on and eyes closed I would listen to musical theatre albums from start to finish. I would go to another place and become someone else.

As soon as was able I was gone, working anywhere and on any stage that would have me.

Working was food. Working was air. Working was people like me.

To not be in a rehearsal room or backstage or onstage or in the green room or even on the subway on the way to work leaves me lost.

But what I really mean to say is that I miss you. I miss everyone.

I miss everyone ever worked with and everyone I haven't worked with yet.

I miss the people I will never work with.

I miss everyone.

I miss food and air.

Let's GO.

Liz
@lizthelarsen
Originally from New Hope, PA

Dear Tara,

When the lights are bright again, your ghost light inside gets a break! It will be like witnessing the Emerald City get her glittering emeralds back again, but this time very much with different eyes, eyes that have swirled in gray complexities for the past yearish, blooming unlikely rainbows even in a staring contest with grief, and now unable to unsee what I was asleep to in "the before time" poppy fields. I have undeniably changed.

I also question if those lights will be for me. I have yet to make my Broadway debut or feel truly a part of this city's theatre community. For all others who feel this way, I see you <3

But I do hold onto the hope of when those lights are indeed bright again, I will feel calls to healing over a hustle, a cacophony of connection to other extraordinary humans my ghost light has missed just like the Scarecrow "most of all."

When the lights are bright again, I now know I will no longer be blinded by them, but finding slippers and a brick road that works for me, and steering those spotlights to hold both our technicolor and our gray.

May those bright lights hold all who want to bask in them.

the good witch of the concrete jungle
@taratagtickles
Originally from Middlesex, NJ

> ## Working was food. Working was air.

Dear Shoba,

When the lights are bright again, and we close out this painful chapter, I want you to look back on everything this time has brought into focus. Remember the value you found in stillness, and the new level of gentleness and care you developed for yourself. Never forget your immense love for what you do, and how when everything was down, the countless ways in which you **continued to push, create and make the world a better place.** I want you to continue to honor your body, a body that has now kept you safe and healthy during a pandemic. **Remember that the shoulders you are lucky to lean on, near and far, are your home.** When you are back on stage, I want you to recognize the tremendous privilege of getting to look into another person's eyes, connect and storytell. Never take for granted any moment in a space where your heart gets to beat in tandem with thousands of others. Remember the importance of speaking up for what is right and equitable and that **kindness and empathy always win.** Lastly, I want you to know that what you do is **essential** to the world, and key to bringing us clarity and healing after this terrible time. If there's anything that this pandemic taught, it's that nothing in life is promised. Live every day doing what you love, and serving the greater good.

Love always,
Shoba
@shoba_narayan

> "Never take for granted any moment in a space where your heart gets to beat in tandem with thousands of others."

HEALING

Dear Sydney Mei,

When the lights are bright again
You will feel the air between
Your hopes and dreams begin
To sizzle with the energy
Of familiar faces
And laughter that traces
The walls, the ropes, the curtains,
The stage, the lights, the seats
The air, the guises, the mirth
The tragedy, the love, the stories
The stories
That bind us together
In this turbulent weather
And make us human.
For what is a human without a story?
What is a story without a character?
What is a character without a community?
Without community nobody sees or hears or feels her.
You're missing the art
The art
Hell, you're missing the chance
To travel the worlds in this world
To have the reason to dance
And don't get me wrong
I know you love your new conspirators
The buzz of freedom calling your name
The trees in your kingdom curing the pain
You're trying things you never have before
But how long will novelty fuel this flame
Before the longing for what is real
Reveals the necessity of what is
Dear Mother Earth, why is the sky blue?
You wake up exhausted from the missing
The missing

Cuz you never know what you're missing
'Til it's dancing in front of you
And that's how you'll know
When the lights are bright again
When you feel the air between
Your hopes and dreams begin
To sparkle with the energy
Of your friends, no–your family
My family
Oh, when the lights are bright again
Oh, when the lights are bright again…

With deep respect for my fellow storytellers
And love for anyone suffering the loss of their livelihood…
their passion,
Sydney Mei
@sydneymei
Originally from Eugene, OR

> ## What is a character without a community?

> ## I will be content in knowing my heart is mending.

Dear Anita-ali,

When the lights are bright again I will be alive again! Not like today when I am low, numb. I will arrive early so I can see my "ghost" light! I will take in the scent of my "person" as places is called. My heart will soar as we both listen to the audience settling down. I will thank God for letting me feel this again. I will smell the smells of live theater and embrace the darkness of backstage. Either limited run or not I will be content in knowing my heart is mending...

I WILL REST WHEN THE LIGHTS ARE BRIGHT AGAIN!

Anita-ali
@StarwranglerAli
Originally from Brooklyn, NY

Dear Lana,

When the lights are bright again, I can't wait to prove myself as an actor. When I first heard about the shutdown, I was well into my last semester of high school, I'd just finished a community theatre production of Grease, and I was set to play the Narrator in my school's spring production, Puffs.

My friend Kelly drove me home after rehearsal, and I got the call... I was super bummed, but quarantine made me think a lot! Not all of it was positive, but I wouldn't want to have done it any other way. Being alone for months on end, not having to be perceived a certain way, it helped me figure out my true feelings. I thought about sexual orientation, gender identity, but most importantly, body image. I always knew it would be tough as a "big girl" in general, but it wasn't until recently that I saw just how fatphobic the industry can be. There's hardly any roles for big women where their weight isn't essential to the plot. I went down a terrible path of self-loathing, I questioned everything I did as an artist. I remember asking myself, "Why should casting directors love me when I can't even love myself?"

Fast forward, about halfway through my first semester in college. I found myself surrounded by just the most kind, supportive people. My classmates, teachers, neighbors! Everyone was hyping up everyone, and I loved it! I never had this kind of support system. It took me a while, but I'm realizing that the most seemingly random thing can be the reason you get cast or not. It's of course about who you know, but it's also how tall you are, what color your hair is, or even if you didn't smile when you walked in. It's of course about what the director has in mind, but that doesn't mean you shouldn't give it your all at an audition. It's your time to show them why you're the right choice. You never know, you might just change their mind.

Holding onto hope,
Lana
@lana.llama02
Originally from Newbury, VT

It allowed you to actually create out of want and delight.

Dear Brittany,

When the lights are bright again, you will look back on this time with gratitude and a knowing of the healing that took place. You are more aligned with who you are and what you're about, because of the collective grief and pause. When you were in bed with Covid, the same day Broadway shut down, you didn't know it at the time but you could've been one of the unlucky ones. You will never allow yourself to be so suffocated in self-doubt, shrinking under the unexpressed shared humanity. The amount of space you take up and joy you claim for yourself and others, will never be self-sabotaged again. It made you slow down. It allowed you to actually create out of want and delight. To trust and surrender to presence. To face all of the ugliness that is racial injustice and systemic oppression. You had to acknowledge your role in privileged self-centeredness and being sooo "busy" with your own shit, that you couldn't even see the weight your friends had been carrying. You will continue to hold everything you are and everything that you have sacred. What hasn't and will never change is how much you love dancing and singing with the people you love. They make you feel the most you. They see something in you that you've never really understood. You will hold them tighter, laugh louder, be more obnoxious in public together, and make sure you're listening when they share their stories of how they made it through this darkness.

P.S. You have a private room karaoke reunion with your people and it's everything. P.S.S. You make your Broadway Debut in the most perfect show for you.

Holding Onto Hope,
Brittany
@bittybohn
Originally from Atlanta, GA

STEPHANIE BISSONNETTE
Originally from
Massena, NY

Dear Stephanie,

When the lights are bright again you will feel the magical power of truly healing. Your struggles will finally feel like they have passed. You will feel the joys of sharing your passion, and what you have trained tirelessly to achieve since you were 5 years old. A dream you manifested and worked for was taken away by this virus. However, this love has always been more than just the shows, the costumes, and the glory. It took away connection. The feeling of sharing a space with other artists. Dance classes filled with poised and perspiring bodies. Sharing the gift of dance and inspiring one another to push a little further, give a little more, and be vulnerable with our stories. You will feel this high again. That feeling of euphoria as you pant from exhausting your limbs from reaching farther, digging deeper, and kicking higher. A glorious release where the world disappears and you can just be. Exist. Free.

Your journey has been filled with ups and downs, as are most epic sagas. You are a survivor in every sense of the word. In 2014, you moved to the greatest city in the world. In 2016, you earned your place in the union by pounding the pavement earning every last point. In 2018, you booked your dream job and helped create a Broadway hit from the very beginning. You worked with people you have idolized for years and finally felt like your moment had arrived. Every dream came true. In 2019, you were faced with your biggest challenge and still managed to come out on top. Fighting back from a cancerous brain tumor to dawn the stage once again. The show was the light at the end of the tunnel. Then in 2020, that dream was once again taken away by disease and fear. Now in 2021 that light at the end of the tunnel has seemed to have been extinguished. The show closed. No hope of returning to Broadway once the pandemic was over. I know this time was incredibly dark. You are a survivor. You always find a way. We all do. We fight to live and dance another day.

When the lights are bright again you will feel that rush of nerves in the wings before the downbeat of the overture. You will start new adventures and meet new people who will inspire you and help you on your journey. The excitement of sitting in an audience and clutching the Playbill as the lights dim. You will be reunited with so many friends, artists and colleagues who have lifted you up in times of hardship and inspired you to keep pushing. You'll be united with those teachers that continued to invest in you even through a computer screen, never giving up on your potential and helping you continue to train. When the lights are bright again you will feel complete. Whole. It will be that opening night curtain call. Only the gratitude and joy will last longer than one night. It will live on every time the music plays and your soul moves you to dance.

Always,
Stephanie
@stephbizz14

> **We fight to live and dance another day.**

Dear KaH LeeB,

When the lights are bright again you will look back on this time of pain, heartache, panic, and fear and somehow find the light in each dark place. It seems such an obscure thought to seek the joy in those moments, but they are there. This has been a chance to heal from old wounds, to love family you never got to see, to spread hope to the other thousands of Broadway family that were dealing with immense stress, and to realize all of the necessary things really weren't. You hit one of the lowest points in your life physically and mentally, but you pressed on and fought for yourself. You didn't give up and for that, be proud. You let faith and trust lead you towards a brighter day and you know that this test was yours to tackle because it opened your heart and gives you the strength to help someone else in the future. To all of my Broadway family, those I've met, and those I'll meet soon, you always have a shoulder to come to and I will always cheer you on. Let's us love one another, lift one another, let us laugh together, cry together, hug, and have after show drinks on a 8 show week. Let us make memories that will last 1000 lifetimes, but most importantly, let us be there for one another.

Never give up, never back down, and always buddies
forever,
KaH LeeB
@thecreativecaleb
Originally from Wausau, FL

> # This has been a chance to heal from old wounds...

Dear Amber,

When the lights are bright again, you will press on as if they were never out. This pandemic will continue to teach you that your own light isn't dependent on a role or job, a close call or an almost, or the ink on your resume. You are a whole person, with a handful of talents, riding out a worldwide trauma. It's all gonna be ok. There is room for your art, even if you take a winding path when everyone else zig zags. There is room for all art and all artists. The world needs us!

Some things to remember:

1. You are still that 15 year old who saw Les Mis on Broadway, and during "Lovely Ladies" thought, THAT IS ME.

2. SWEATPANTS are the only "costume" you need. Leggings are now considered dressing up. And underwire has become obsolete. Bye underwire.

3. Just "hanging in there" has been, and is, enough. (Thank you Michael Rodriguez @ The Roster).

4. Keep singing.

5. Your Broadway debut is still possible.

6. Theater needed a metamorphosis. Perhaps we all did.

7. That college teacher wasn't kidding when he said "this biz will be a marathon, not a sprint". Coronavirus, life, our industry-run steady, not fast.

8. You don't need that high C.

9. Following your dreams has been a dream in itself. And as your mom says "it's the journey, not the destination". Start listening to her, ok?

10. Love you.

Xo
Amber
@ambertaryncarson
Originally from all over the USA

> ## Will the church bells ever ring out for us?

Dear Valerie,

When the lights are bright again, you're going to be a bit numb. You'll do what you always do; take in the moment, breathe and then turn back to the work you were most likely doing on your laptop for whatever Zoom reading you're facilitating that week. You'll write in the Variations Facebook group a message and most likely receive text messages from the fam. And then, later that night, you'll most likely be lying in bed in the dark when the questions hits you:

Will the bells ring out for us?

On the day Biden was projected to win the presidency, the city screamed with joy. Horns were honked, pots and pans were banged on from the windows, people were crying in the streets. And church bells rang out.

But when Broadway announces shows can start rehearsals again, putting thousands of people back to work and essentially restarting our economy, will the city celebrate with us? Or will they expect us to just smile and wave? Or shut up and dance? Or ignore that EVERYONE who has ever worked on a stage was massively affected by this?

Does the show actually go on?

Will the church bells ever ring out for us?

I think the answer you'll find in the dark is: Maybe.

And as for you, babe, never forget 2020. You're numb... but you're going to be ok.

xxx,
Valerie
@valeriecaniglia1
Originally from Denville, NJ

Dear Ta'Nika,

When the lights are bright again I will rejoice because I will finally be able to do what I love, what I was called in this world to do. Every time I step onto the stage, I will remember how I dreamed of that moment for an entire year as I grieved the loss of my career, passion, and community. When the lights are bright again I will be filled with gratitude that I get to use my talents to speak truth and inspire anyone who watches. When the lights are bright again I will finally feel like myself again, creating and making art and music with amazing artists. When the lights are bright again the world and I will be one step closer to being healed.

Ta'Nika Gibson
@tanika_renee_gibson
Originally from Springfield, MA

Dear Meghan,

When the lights are bright again....I will fight for my dreams the way I've fought for my life throughout this year. When life stopped and the industry completely shut down, I thought I was going to be sitting around waiting for my life to begin again. Man, I was so wrong. This pandemic quite literally saved my life. While we've all been anxiously awaiting for our industry to return, I was diagnosed with Breast Cancer at the age of 26. Going through this during a global pandemic was not what I had planned. When the lights are bright again, I will walk back into every audition room having kicked cancer's ass, and with more fire in me than ever before.

Love always,
Meghan
@meghangratzer
Originally from Queens, NY

Dear Amber,

When the lights are bright again...
Scratch that
The lights were never dimmed
We are the light
It is inside of every one of us
For far too long, this industry and the white supremacy and racism
that controls it
did everything in its power to dim our light
to make us feel small
to quiet our voices
to bend and break us

I have watched the light leave the eyes of people that I love
because they got tired of fighting
and screaming
and advocating
and pleading

They grew tired of trying to make space for themselves in an
industry that was not made with them in mind
An industry that was built on their backs and stole their shine
their smile
their music
their movement
their joy

When the pandemic closed our doors
and we had time to rest
and heal
and love on ourselves
I saw a light in my community that I had never seen before
I saw lights shining brighter than they'd ever shone
I saw those lights giving themselves permission to be...
light

When Broadway returns, I hope we never look back
I hope we remember the discomfort
the pain
the embarrassment
the weight

And then the pivot
the expansion
the growth and the glory

> ❝ The lights were
> never dimmed
> We are the light. ❞

I hope we never wait on anyone to give us permission to be bold
and BAD
and fearless
and unapologetic
ever again

When Broadway returns
We will build our own tables
We will rebuild our communities
We will talk less and listen more
We will invest in each other
We will divest from toxic, harmful, and racist people
and organizations
We will continue to do the work.

Amber
@amberiman_
Originally from Atlanta, GA

L MORGAN LEE
Originally from
Bowie, MD

Dear L Morgan,

When the lights are bright again don't forget all that you have learned. Continue to ask yourself the questions that scare you...lean into them. Generations of people have fought, marched, died, loved, lived for you to have the privileges that so many of us take for granted. Remember that and continue to do your part, no matter how big or small, in making our industry, and more importantly our world, a better place for those coming up behind us. There is somewhere a little girl that will find you, that will one day see your steps, and know that because you travel this road and have survived, she will be able to as well. Continue to dream - both because duh, manifestation is real but also, because that little girl needs to know that it's possible. That it's ok to dream. Who are we kidding? We all need to know that sometimes.

When the lights are bright again, remember that your life still matters, even after the dust has settled and folx are no longer hashtagging or sharing their allyship on Instagram stories. There are many who genuinely want to evolve and much like all of us, are still figuring out how...remember that and try to meet people where they are. Some relationships have faded, while others have grown...make sure to let those closest to you know how much you love and appreciate them. Give them their flowers. They are incredible humans. Cherish every moment you have with them. Also, don't stop going to your rooftop to breathe and take in the views above the city. It's beautiful. It's peaceful. And finally, please remember that when the lights are bright again, you are enough. Wherever you are in your journey. Whatever your body. Whatever your level of drive. Whether you get the job or not. However you're feeling. You. Are. Enough.

Love,
The You that made it through
@lmorganlee

"...don't stop going to your rooftop to breathe..."

Dear Jerusha,

When the lights are bright again, I'm not even sure you'll really notice.

It's not because you don't care. You do.

I'm sure the group texts are going to be blowing up, drinks are going to be had. You'll probably find yourself in midtown somewhere dancing in the streets, making your way to Haswell Green's for a nightcap. Bliss.

But then you'll pause. You'll go sit down. Deep breath. You will not be returning to your dream as the same person you were in 2019.

Your light turned back on this January. 2021. You did that.

It took time.

The pursuit of happiness is often unaccompanied by joy.

I hate that he had to break you down that way. Why must we bruise to heal?

You spent almost two years and the entirety of quarantine with someone, just to find out it was all a lie.

What then, is truth?

What is your truth??

You can still hear echos of yourself sobbing on the bathroom floor with the lights off, thinking that if you did in the dark, you wouldn't have to face yourself. But the law of physics states that light still exists, even in the dark. Those echos used to make you cringe and feel shame. But now when you hear them you just think of strength.

And that strength is how you found your worth.

So you'll be happy when the lights are bright again, because collective light will bring about an abundance of joy for all.

But your light, your why?

It's already on.

I know there will be seasons in which you experience doubt, fear, pain, & sadness.

But now you know that you don't have to face them in the dark.

There is no lane. There is no right way. There is just YES and NOW.

So here's to the clapping at 7pm, may we always be cheering for each other.

Jerusha
@jerushacavazos
Originally from Celebration, FL

> "You will not be returning to your dream as the same person you were in 2019."

Dear Beth,

When the lights are bright again everything will be different. A year ago you were at a place in this business that you'd worked toward for 17 years, and it had paid off! Three national tours in one year, a principal contract, going on as Dolly understudying Betty Buckley, finally convincing one particular casting agency to like you... you had three jobs lined up and the spaces between jobs had lessened and the jobs were things that you were truly excited about! And then it all stopped. And while many friends and colleagues "pivoted" it only showed you more how much you wanted to perform, how this life was still it for you. So you went to live with family and met your two new nieces and everything was on pause for awhile. Until you felt a lump. And then suddenly the year wasn't about missing theatre, it was about having cancer. And people keep saying, "Well this is actually perfect timing" because you're not missing any Broadway jobs! And now, you're just praying every day that when the lights are bright again you'll be healthy and whole and done with treatment. You'll have a little less boob (not too much though, because cleavage is your favorite accessory onstage), less lymph nodes, less hair from chemo, maybe less energy, but not everything will be lost. You'll have more passion, more perspective, and more confidence. You'll take the feeling from every zoom with every high school across America that you've done - the one where you're jazzed and hopeful and reminded truly WHY we do this and you'll bring it into the room and onto the stage. And then you'll tell the story, you'll brighten people's nights, you'll put a song in their heart and teach them a lesson over two hours that makes the world a better place. Because we've lost a lot of people this year but you're not going anywhere, and the lights will be bright again before you know it. Don't give up hope!

Love,
Beth
@bethkirkp
Originally from Cincinnati, OH

> " **Don't give up hope!** "

HOPE

Dear Jessie,

When the lights are bright again where will you fit in? Will you start back up where you left off?! On the high of working a long stint, but also tired from just closing your two year run of a show? Will you be finding your stride in the room like before? Will you be getting seen and being heard?! Or will you be behind? Lost in the background? What even is "behind" anymore? I'm not sure.

Will people care about the things they posted about this summer?! Will Black lives REALLY matter? Will you REALLY be seen? Will you REALLY be heard? Will the change that's needed to happen for so long REALLY come?! Or will it be lost in the background? Will it be lost in the brightness of the lights? Will it be lost in the "excitement of being back"?! I'm not sure.

I am sure that when the lights are bright again we all will be able to see clearly- the good and the not so good. We will have a chance to fix and change. When the lights are bright again, questions will have to be answered.

I am curious to know what you will see. I am curious to know what you will hear. The answers given will lead you to where you fit. The answers given will lead you to where you will go.

If this time has shown you anything, Jessie, it's that life is too short to not demand to be seen-to demand to be heard. There is a place for you and those answers you need- just like there is for everyone else.

Love your higher self (aka.. you)
Jessie Hooker-Bailey
@JessieHookerBailey
Originally from Wilkes-Barre, PA

> ## Will the change that's needed to happen for so long REALLY come?!

Dear Fran

When the lights are bright again you will be back in NYC. If you aren't backstage working you will be in the house for some show's first performance. There is no WAY you will miss that moment; that phenomenal once in a lifetime sound of people applauding as the lights go to half for the first time since March 2020. The applause and cheering, not just for Broadway returning, but the acknowledgement that we have all made it through this horrifying nightmare. That moment of recognition will go on and on and they should let it, because I know people will be crying on both sides of the curtain. It is going to be like an opening night on steroids and I can't freaking wait.

Until then keep loving your chosen family.
Fran
@girlfranjewelry
Originally from Steamwood, IL

Dear Lo,

When the lights are bright again, I promise it will fill your cup. I promise your voice will be heard, I promise your light will be seen.

Baby, don't give up. You are meant to change the world- through a laugh, through a song, through a meeting. When the lights are bright again, so will your heart be.

Never again will your efforts go unnoticed, unappreciated, un-anything. It will be, everything.

You will rise, we will rise, from the nothingness leftover to the beauty of what is, can, and will be.

You were meant for this. Don't forget it.
Lauren
@laurenwags
Originally from Yorktown Heights, NY

Dear Shannon,

When the lights are bright again, I hope you never lose the sparkle you found amidst the darkness. I hope you see the value you bring to the world in ADDITION to the beautiful talents that you have to share and collaborate with on and off stage. I hope this painful and sadness filled time of separation from your community proves time and time again that you belong, are worthy, and are by NO means defined by a job or career. I hope you allow your sparkle to enter the room and understand that it is the key to unlocking everything you wish for in your life. I hope you hold close to your heart your Broadway debut family – and honor Nick Cordero in all of your work. Life is too short to not let your true self shine. Be strong yet soft, be loud yet humble and lead with love, never fear.

Love,
Shannon
@smullen312
Originally from Rochester, NY

Dear Sara,

When the lights are bright again I hope I feel more alive than I have this past year. I hope that little flame in my gut is ignited again and turned on high!

To be honest, there has been a lot of feeling numb about our business this year. I kept my head down and just kept moving....or not moving while binging the new true crime doc that was released on Netflix. (There was a LOT of not moving while binging.) I found myself shutting down a bit watching all of these incredible "pandemic pivots" from fellow artists. Even feeling a little jealous that they had other loves and passions they were diving into. I thought to myself, "I genuinely do not have a clue what I would pivot to, and I DON'T WANT TO PIVOT, I WANT TO PERFORM!" Those were the temper tantrum feelings circling my brain as 2020 progressed. Instead of getting all caught up in those intense feelings though, I turned them off, and I felt nothing. Survival mode I guess. I've always been pretty good at adapting to change and creating new normals, which I think in general is a helpful skill to have. However, in this case, it allowed me to turn off this flame inside me. My passion. She went to sleep, and I missed her. A LOT.

Something has shifted though in the last month or so. I'm not even sure what. Spring? More sunlight? Vaccines? I think it's probably a lot of those things, but I can feel that little fire in my belly again. I can feel that anticipation of something new, something unknown. I can feel a little glimmer of hope. I keep thinking that if I'm feeling some hope NOW, then when the lights are bright again, my hope for this industry, this career, this PASSION of mine will be too great to contain. I CAN'T WAIT.

With love,
Sara
@shepnailsit
Originally from Toledo, OH

> " I hope that little flame in my gut is ignited again... "

Dear Suri,

When the lights are bright again, you will be back on that Broadway stage performing live. The pandemic has taught you to never lose hope in life. It was truly devastating to see the lights shut down. But, they will never be like that forever. The lights will always be bright in your heart, no matter what happens. Being on that stage is your passion. You will live your dream. There are many negative outcomes from the pandemic but always think of the positives. Even though the pandemic has stopped you from performing live, it will never stop you from performing. Work on improving your acting, dancing, and singing in the pandemic. This is the time to improve your craft and be ready for when the lights are bright again. When the lights are bright again, you will come out of the pandemic as a stronger and better person.

Holding on to hope, love, and a bright future,
Suri Marrero
@surimarrero

> "The lights will always be bright in your heart..."

Dear James,

So...How are you? It's been just over one year since the beginning of a change we could not have foreseen. It's also the day after the 2nd anniversary of your show that made you a principal after 19 years on Broadway. You're on the subway sitting across from a guy eating a sandwich. On the subway. In this pandemic (James put your actual left eyebrow down).

How am I? Blessed. I am aware of the state of the world. I am also fully aware of my situation. My needs are met. My health is good (aside from you eating like you're still doing 8 shows a week James!) My family and chosen family are also well. I am blessed.

Also.

I do have anger...
Fear...
Sadness...
Regret...
Uncertainty...

At times I have been in that couch (yes IN it) and my bed for days. So much beyond my control. I try to step through it with positivity, to lead with love. But–I am human. Still, I am grateful for the unexpected beauty this difficult time has brought and I hold on to those things. I try.

> **That fire that has become embers will be stoked.**

Change. It's irregular waves ebb, flow, and at times crash. I miss my showbiz family so much. I believe we are the true heartbeat of NYC. The lights have been dim on the houses that we represent. But dim does not mean off. **You can never turn off art.** No. You can never completely darken creativity and it's spirit for then the world would be without light.

We have lost some luminous lights that we never imagined we would. Yes. That makes my heart heavy at times, but our lights are still connected. When the lights are bright again? That fire that has become embers will be stoked. When we are able to commune those flames will catch. When our bodies move, words issue forth, and voices soar the intensity will increase. When musicians are set and stitches are checked. When tickets touch the hands of our congregation and their presence fills our second homes. When seats are filled, announcements are made and voices hush. When that curtain does finally rise–ALL our lights will join and burn brighter than ever before!

When the lights go bright again–we will be home.

Love,
You
@ijamesharkness

Dear New Mama; lost in the pandemic,

> **You have learned to let go, and to fight, to be truly in solitude, with a new human.**

When the lights are bright again remember to keep the grace and self-love you have earned during this time. You fled your beloved city, swollen, bruised, with your cesarean scar painful and oozing; your 2 week old baby boy tucked into his newborn car seat. Your mother in law drove you and your new family of 3 upstate to keep safe and get away from the busy streets of Queens. Right when lockdown started. You learned to breastfeed, painfully, you wondered if you would ever sleep again, lose the weight, audition... or be the you, you knew. All in your sister in law's childhood bedroom. The NYTimes app on your iPhone was your companion at 3 am while you fed your baby boy, grieving the seemingly lost city. When every article headline was terrifying, when you questioned why you had bothered to pursue the path you have always known – as it all seemed lost. You forced yourself to do a self-tape at 6 weeks postpartum just to prove you could still "do it all." Bloated and exhausted; you did not book the job. But remember you came back. Back to the city you love, back with a healthy – now 1 year old – back to fitness, back to auditions, and even gained perspective for a career pivot, and even better, side hustle that serves. As the pandemic has taught you that one needs to be able to pivot in life and not grasp so tightly to what you thought would be... or should be... or more importantly what you thought others thought you should be . You have learned to let go, and to fight, to be truly in solitude, with a new human. The world is not fair to women and it has in many ways been the hardest year of your life, but you haven't receded; holding out hope that you and the world can grow, heal, and remember never to take the little things for granted ever again. Once the lights are bright again, you will come back, and there will always be a bright day to look to.

With love,
New mama; lost in the pandemic
@jacquelineraywegman
Originally from Malta, NY

Dear Seth,

When the lights are bright again, how we will rejoice!

Remember how at the first preview of *Love Quirks*, the audience stopped the show three times and gave it a standing ovation? It was the culmination of a decade of development and fundraising to realize the dream of bringing the show off-Broadway. So many friends came to celebrate that night, and it will go down as one of, if not the best, birthdays of my life.

Two weekends of bliss followed as the glowing reviews spread! As the third weekend approached, the anxiety over whether or not to cancel permeated. One by one friends said they couldn't come to see the show because of the viral "viral" concerns. How we struggled with the decision to cancel performances and postpone the upcoming opening night party. Then there was the depressing task of informing out-of-town friends and Broadway celebrities the opening was off for now.

Fear. Anxiety. Depression. Anger. Denial. A circle of emotions that felt like a perverted wheel of fortune. I kept convincing myself the show would reopen by summer, then fall, then early 2021…

The year still had its good moments. I proposed to my girlfriend, and she said yes! I produced 130 virtual performances! Through the virtual showcase series, I worked with 232 singers from 35 states and 7 countries! I wrote a song cycle chronicling my feelings, and we recorded the *Love Quirks* original off-Broadway cast album!

I learned many life lessons. I worked on gratefulness. I spent time with my cat, Smee. I tried to learn patience. I learned to let go of uncontrollable things like deadlines and timelines. I read over 70 books, watched 100 operas, studied Japanese, and played virtual chess.

Finally, I have learned not to take things for granted. When I can be on stage performing live cabaret again, and when the opening night curtain goes up on *Love Quirks* off-Broadway, it will be more special than before. I have been through the storm, and have come out drenched, but still alive.

Fondly,
Seth
@sethbhdotcom
Originally from New York, NY

Dear Ashley,

When the lights are bright again, I hope you'll know that you belong here, that you are not, in fact, an imposter, and it was so much more than just "luck" that you landed where you landed. You worked hard. You were kind. You pushed when it was difficult and you cried when it let you down, but you never gave up. You earned this: celebrate that.

When the lights are bright again, say a quiet thank you to all the turns of fate and all the sweat that brought you here, because these lights really have saved your life. It was the knowledge that they'd be back that kept you going when the road felt its darkest this last year. You drew strength from the community, YOUR community, knowing you were all in this together, and most important of all, that you were not ever alone.

When the lights are bright again, remember that while this is a large part of you, it is not all of you. Remember that you are more than the work that you do when the house lights go down and the curtain rises. Remember that the community you've built in those wings continues on beyond the walls, and the friends and family you've found eight times a week are still there when the lights go dark. Remember all you learned this past year, remember the joy of stepping back into the theater for the first time, remember the magic; that same magic and joy brought the lights back, and will keep them burning bright, long after you take your final bow.

We can't know what's around the next turn, but we can greet it with open arms and know, no matter what, that the lights will always return.

Keep going,
Ashley
@ashleyjotimm
Originally from Bladen, NE

ALI STROKER
Originally from
Ridgewood, NY

Dear Ali,

When the lights are bright again, remember there's no going back. Move forward with the confidence to make change, with a renewed sense of gratitude for what we do onstage. Love and cherish every moment that you have in front of an audience.

Remember your love to be seen and to connect with the audience. Let your light shine even when you're afraid or in pain.

Remember to always speak your truth and stand behind the people who need you most. Sometimes being a leader means staying quiet while others have the microphone.

Remember the moments you sang to your laptop while hundreds of kids watched from homes they could barely leave for a year.

Remember the zoom readings, the zoom concerts, and sharing your tears with the people you trusted and loved most.

Treasure the quiet moments. They can sometimes be the most special of all.

We've all now learned that the most uncomfortable situations can bring out the most impactful change. You must not be the last of "the firsts." The theater community is the greatest in the world when we fight for each other and for Equality.

Here's to a new season and a new chapter of theatre HISTORY.

It's up to us!

Ali
@AliStroker

> **Love and cherish every moment that you have in front of an audience.**

"Keep Hope Alive."

Dear Irene,

When the lights are bright again… I will take my working on Broadway over 50 years behind the scenes as a African-American press agent/producer more seriously and realize the commitment I must have to ALL of my theatrical community and friends and will be any means necessary "Keep Hope Alive."

When the lights are bright again there go I.

Irene
@iamirenegandy

IRENE GANDY

Dear Hannah,

When the lights are bright again, you will probably cry. Ok scratch that. You will DEFINITELY cry. Weep, in fact – big fat tears rolling down your cheeks. They will be tears for your ten-year-old self in her very first production of Anything Goes at Characters & Company, where they inexplicably added a children's chorus even though it made absolutely no sense. They will be for the last time you were on stage-filling Trina's shoes and feeling like you were finally coming into your own as a grounded, adult woman after years of feeling like you didn't quite fit. And they will be for your future, for your dreams of what might be, for the hopes that one day you will finally get to fulfill your lifelong dream of being Fanny Brice.

Don't get me wrong, it's still going to be freaking hard. You were not on Broadway when everything shut down, and frankly, who knows if you will ever get there. But there will be hope, there will be possibility, there will be the tingly anticipation of whatever opportunity is barrelling around the corner. No matter what, you will continue to seek the joy – oh that palpable, soul shaking joy – of making an audience laugh, of finding a moment of connection with a new castmate, of breaking through a barrier of your own making in the rehearsal room.

Oh Hannah, that ten-year-old you, that awkward, shy girl with a Jew-fro and a love for Judy Garland, she is BEGGING you to keep going, to stick in, to not give up. Please keep her with you and hold her hand until the lights are bright again.

Hannah
@KiemlikeTime
Originally from St. Louis, MO

> **I hope they shine on more and more people who look like you and those around you.**

Dear Kamilah,

When the Lights are Bright Again, they will find you in a new city, with a new job, at a new theater, doing the things that you've trained your whole life for. Like the unexpected twist of this pandemic that caused us all to pivot, reimagine and rededicate ourselves to the work, your career took a sharp turn in 2020. It was not a traditional path; it did not look the way you thought it would – but Literary Managers don't often look like you. When the lights are bright again, I hope that they find our entire industry changed, much in the ways you have changed in this last year. They will find our spaces more open and inclusive, they will find our community more thoughtful, careful and engaged, they will find that there is more time than we think there is to get down to the business of being alive.

When the lights are bright again, I hope they shine on more and more people who look like you and those around you. Black. Indigenous. Latine. Asian. Queer. Beautiful. All shapes, sizes, genders, abilities. May the lights, when they are bright again, shine like the sun on us all.

This is not the first time theater has had to go underground in this way, and it will likely not be the last, but hopefully like all those times in history, we will see a revolution in its return!

Kamilah
@writingthewrong
Originally from Gastonia, NC

Dear *Jennafer,*

When the lights are bright again, you will realize that they never completely went out. These countless days, weeks, and months will be dark in their own right. And in this time you will be forced to sit in the darkness. Don't be afraid to sit in it.

Be still.

Lament.

Cry out.

Mourn what was lost.

Mourn what never was.

But don't you be afraid to look the darkness straight in the face. Because here's a secret--one you can carry into the darkness with you: the darkness, no matter how dark, can never drown out the light. And Jennafer, there is a light in you. Look around--there is light everywhere.

Remember when you stood in a dark theatre and gazed upon the beauty of the ghost light, observing how even the smallest light can illuminate the darkest of places. Be not afraid.

When the lights are bright again, Jennafer, it will not take long for your eyes to adjust and you will know that the Light was there all along.

The only way forward is through.

Do justice, love kindness, walk humbly.

Jennafer
@jennafernewberry
Originally from Houston, TX

> ...the darkness, no matter how dark, can never drown out the light.

Dear *JM,*

When the lights are bright again you will always remember. In the 80's when AIDS came to take the lives of so many friends and family fighting for life, it was being supported by your community that gave you hope.

In Sept. 2001 9/11 devastated our city, but it was our community that stood together and refused to hide or live in fear that gave us all hope.

Now COVID -19 has forced you to live in isolation for more than a year from friends , family , loved ones, your entire community. The loss of life will be unfathomable. In the darkness and isolation of this pandemic you will find ways, new ways to stay connected. You will laugh, cry, march, vote, listen and engage even in isolation.

Then when the time comes, and it will come, you must take what you have heard, learned and seen and share it. Rally the troops. The entire community that fought AIDS, the entire community that refused to live in fear after 9/11 is the community you so love support and cherish.

Your community needs YOU! Without community we are all isolated, pandemic or no pandemic. EVERYONE must know they are part of the community. Everyone must FEEL they are included in the community. BUILD BACK a more inclusive, more connected and more engaged community. Then and only then will we all be able to live FULLOUT!

xo,
JM
@jammyprod
Originally from Paw Paw, MI

> You will laugh, cry, march, vote, listen and engage even in isolation.

Dear Jaime,

" I hope that your trans sisters and brothers stand next to you under those lights ... "

When the lights are bright again, I hope they shine down on a million black and brown faces.

I hope that one of those black and brown faces is yours.

I hope that you understand your worth as an artist has nothing to do with your resume.

I hope that you understand the truth of what it means to be a part of a community.

I hope that you understand that you are fit to lead.

I hope that you understand that you are fit to speak.

I hope that you understand that your voice is and has always been your most powerful weapon.

I hope that you return to the creation of art with a renewed sense of purpose.

Lastly, I hope that your trans sisters and brothers stand next to you under those lights and I hope that they reflect them so brightly it is blinding.

I hope you know you can make a difference.

Ase
@papimagic

REMEMBER

Dear Lynda,

When the lights are bright again, don't forget...

Don't forget the feeling of shock when you received the email cancelling your 6 month contract that you had just left all of your in-school teaching residences for because it made you wake up and remember that you can't control everything.

Don't forget that yes, you were going to be in this for a while and would have to teach on this thing called Zoom because it made you try something new and uncomfortable, and you can do that and be okay.

Don't forget the fear you felt journeying outside of your apartment for the first time in three weeks to your grocery store two blocks away in a double mask and gloves because it makes every brave step you take through these vibrant city streets that much more empowering.

Don't forget the endless variety of at-home workouts in your living room because they kept you moving in more ways than one.

Don't forget sitting on a step-stool in your kitchen reading and listening to podcasts for hours in the middle of the day because it allowed you to find, cherish, and look forward to the simple joys, like quiet time with just you and a fabulous story.

Don't forget not singing for 3 months because it felt forced and too sad because that space was needed and now singing feels spiritual again.

Don't forget the day you decided that you could and would do everything you said you would do this year, but it would just have to look differently than you imagined and you were okay with that because it reminded you that you are adaptable.

Don't forget recording your original music in your home studio – aka your living room – in the middle of New York City August, with no AC, because that's badass commitment, babe.

Don't forget teaching 20 people in 3 different states in the span of 5 hours from your living room piano bench because even though it was in front of a screen, you turned circumstances into opportunity.

Don't forget feeling like you weren't doing enough to "make the best of this time" because it made you really answer "What do I REALLY want to do with my time?"

> ...never take for granted every breath ever again.

Don't forget sobbing as you walked from the Upper East Side, up 5th Avenue to Harlem after yet another one of your best friends moved from the city because it reminds you that relationships aren't about face time, but quality time, and it's okay to care a fucking lot.

Don't forget the ambulance sirens every 15 minutes for months and months because you've never been more grateful and will never take for granted every breath ever again.

Don't forget getting to know yourself again.

Don't forget one second of this time and these lessons. It's not that you have to actively carry this all with you every day. In fact, don't - because that's a lot, sister! No, you don't have to remember to remember because... it's all a part of you now. You who, after all of that, are much more grateful, adaptable, resourceful, creative, empowered, capable, and ready to step center stage when the lights are bright again.

Love you,
Lynda
@lyndamonsterr
Originally from Henderson, NV

Dear Adena,

When the lights are bright again, remember that feeling at the peak of your career before the lights went out- tap into it, and soar. As you continue to pursue your dreams, it is important to take every moment of the time the lights were dark with you. Don't take for granted the things you discovered that aided you during that time. Allow your body time to rest when it needs to. It is okay to take a day- self care is just as important as the hustle and grind. Remember the community you found from taking class on Zoom in your living room, and how much you couldn't wait to get back and dance in a real studio with your old and new friends! As strange as the circumstances were, be grateful for the time you were given to spend with your family. Bit by bit your career and life as you knew it fell apart, but you gained so much inner strength. **Do not lose what was so hard to find.** Remember that you are always enough, and take that confidence and strength into every audition room with you. Be proud of yourself for continuing on your path, wherever it may lead you. When opportunity knocks and the hustle begins again, let your passion propel you forward. When you step back on a stage, a wave of emotions will come over you, and I know it will ignite a new flame within you. Continue to train, to learn, to grow, to connect with others, and to smile while spreading joy and light. When the lights are bright again, find the good in that wild time, and hold onto it. Everything happens for a reason. Be proud of the obstacles you overcame, and continue to share your story, because when the lights are bright again, the possibilities will be endless.

Stay strong, keep your head up, your heart full, and never stop moving.

Love and light,
Adena
@aershow
Originally from West Orange, NJ

> Remember that you are always enough and take that confidence and strength into every audition room with you.

Dear Brittany,

When the lights are bright again, may you never take for granted the essence of time and the simplicity of being present.

May you remember your resilience to adapt in the face of adversity, trauma, and the changes life has thrown at you – not only in your career, but also in your personal life with the loss of your Dad.

May you remember the strength and trust you've found within yourself to accept the new pathway and reality that has been presented to you.

May you remember that this, in turn, has allowed you to soften and go through grief, realizations, growth, and finding the courage to sit in the unknown.

May you remember that your worth is not solely your career and there is so much depth to you.

May you remember not to identify with the roles that you are given, but by the character of your being.

May you remember the positives that this time away from your career has given you: time with your family, time with your fiancé, time with your closest friends, and most importantly, time with yourself.

May you remember to be grateful for what you have, the body you are within, and the tribe of people you surround yourself with.

May you remember to never take for granted the ability to perform on a Broadway stage again or be in a room filled with incredible artists.

May you remember the impact you have made on the future artists you're teaching and remember the joy you found in watching them grow week-to-week in discovering themselves and their talents.

May you remember to strive, persevere, and put good into the universe!

May you remember to always acknowledge this tumultuous time and remember the hope you had for the future of theatre and the lights being bright again.

May you remember to continue to dream because that is how you got to where you are today.

May you remember to ALWAYS live life to the fullest, just like your Dad.

May you always remember to smile, feel, laugh, and be in the present moment, for that is the only moment that we have.

Love, Light, Hope, and
Laughs,
Brittany
@brittconigatti

"May you remember to be grateful for what you have, the body you are within, and the tribe of people you surround yourself with."

Dear Nick,

When the lights are bright again, may you never forget the lessons that you have learned during this chapter of your life. You have been changed. You have evolved. You have grown.

Remember how you felt before the world got turned upside down. You were experiencing major burnout, questioning your future in the industry, and slowly falling out of love with this art form that has brought you so much joy since you were a child. Who knew that fleeing New York and quarantining in your childhood bedroom for months would help you fall back in love with theatre? Endless days of watching past Tony Awards performances, old movie musicals and shaky recordings of long-lost Broadway shows allowed you to enjoy the art without all of the added stress that this business can dump on you. When the lights are bright again and that stress returns, remember why you love theatre so much.

When the lights are bright again, be proud of how you handled the challenges you faced during this time. You lost your livelihood and created new opportunities that allowed you to grow. Those opportunities did not come easily though. **Never forget how long you sat in a pit of self-doubt before taking action. Never forget the overwhelming support you received once you decided to take action.** When the lights are bright again, never allow yourself to waste time sitting in that place of self-doubt. You are capable. You are intelligent. You are enough.

If you would've told pre-pandemic Nick that he would use this time to build an online community of over fifty thousand theatre loving people and that would then inspire him to start a successful podcast where he interviews Broadway stars every week, he would have laughed right in your face. That is the silver lining in all of this though. We never know when the universe will challenge us to step outside of our comfort zones and uncover new parts of ourselves. When the lights are bright again, don't be afraid to take those steps because when you allow your life to fall into monotony, that is when you start to fall out of love with the things that bring you joy.

When the lights are bright again, remember the commitment you made to yourself. Be a part of the change in this industry. Use your privilege to lift up the voices of the unheard. Use your platform to create opportunities for those who don't have any. Speak up when you see injustice. When the lights are bright again, may they shine on a new beginning for this community.

Be kind to yourself,
Nick
@nickferrao | @BwayBelters
Originally from New York, NY

> "You are capable. You are intelligent. You are enough."

Dear Princess Almost,

When the lights are bright again, you will live out your dream. The time had come to find your light and do what you were once afraid to desire...and then it disappeared. Years of work had finally paid off and you were ready to let it lift your head higher. Yet the stage is not the only place to claim your title. Your inner world is what allowed a kingdom to flourish and you are even more set up to thrive than you were before. You have found strength, resilience, and patience while locked in your tower. **You have found your power and remembered your worth.** Your gown is waiting for you, Princess. Yet now you'll wear it like a Queen. Have faith and trust that one day you will be covered in pixie dust. Your time will come once again, I promise.

Holding onto hope,
Princess Almost
@jennythefoof
Originally from Durham, NH

> **You have found your power and remembered your worth.**

Dear Michaelah Reynolds,

When the lights are bright again, remember the growth you went through during this shutdown. You officially came into the Broadway community in January 2020 doing a completely different job. Losing that job and this community hurt a lot. It felt like you lost everything you built towards in the last two years. But it also gave you the time and passion to pursue photography in the theatre space like you've wanted to for so many years now. This time brought incredible loss, but also revitalized your love for photography, theater, and this community. You've found your creative voice, met many new colleagues, and made some amazing new friends. **When the lights are bright again, you won't be the same person that went into the shutdown, and that's an amazing thing.** Remember your strength because you're just getting started!

Love,
Michaelah Reynolds
@michaelah.jpg
Originally from San Antonio TX

> Remember your strength because you're just getting started!

Dear Amanda,

When the lights are bright again, remember this moment. Right here, right now, writing this letter to yourself when it has been more than a year from your last paid performance. Remember how difficult this time was, but also the recall, the clarity, and reassurance it brought that this is what you are meant to do in your life. Remember the joy you felt any chance you got to dance- even if it was virtually. Remember how fulfilled you felt teaching students from all over the country and watching them progress and achieve their goals. Remember the ache you felt to return to the stage. Remember how you longed for the moment to be standing in your 3 inch character heels for hours on end with blisters and muscle pains. Remember the notes of encouragement throughout this difficult time from family and friends. Remember the hope you have for the future of the arts and the change it needs to propel. **Remember the fight we must continue in order to find equity in our profession.**

As much as you want to forget the pain of this year and move on never to look back…don't. You must remember; and then remember to cherish every second of the lights being on again.

Never losing this gratitude,
Amanda LaMotte
@tinylamotte

AMANDA LAMOTTE
Originally from
New York, NY

AMANDA LAMOTTE

Dear Kenneth,

When the lights are bright again, you will most likely be sobbing uncontrollably from pure and utter happiness.

You will remember being in Fayetteville, AK, about to head to the theater when you found out about the shutdown. Two weeks. Two weeks and then we would all be back.

Now, over a year later, so much has changed, but your love and appreciation for theater sure hasn't. If anything - it has grown immensely.

When you walk into a theater for the first time, you will be overwhelmed with many emotions and memories. You will remember watching your first Broadway show *(Beauty and the Beast)* and thinking how much you wanted to do this when you grew up. You will remember getting the phone call that you were going to be making your Broadway debut. You will remember crying tears of joy as you stood in your final pose of the opening number on the night of your Broadway debut. You will remember the sound of a roaring applause as you finished one of the hardest ballets you have ever danced on a professional stage. You will remember the feeling and excitement of watching your talented friends make their Broadway debuts. You will remember the panic of having to pack last minute on a Monday before a travel day. You will remember the feeling of locking eyes with your family and best friend, Jessica, as you bowed every time they came to see you in a show. You will remember the lifelong friends you have made over your professional career because of theater. You will remember that those were the friends you talked to every day since the shutdown. You will remember that we were all in this together, and that the day is finally here. We are back and we are stronger than ever.

You will get to watch your beautiful friends perform onstage again.

You will perform again.

We will all perform again.

> *Merde,*
> **Kenneth**
> @kennethhmichael
> Originally from Sayville, NY

> "Now over a year later so much has changed, but your love and appreciation for theatre sure hasn't."

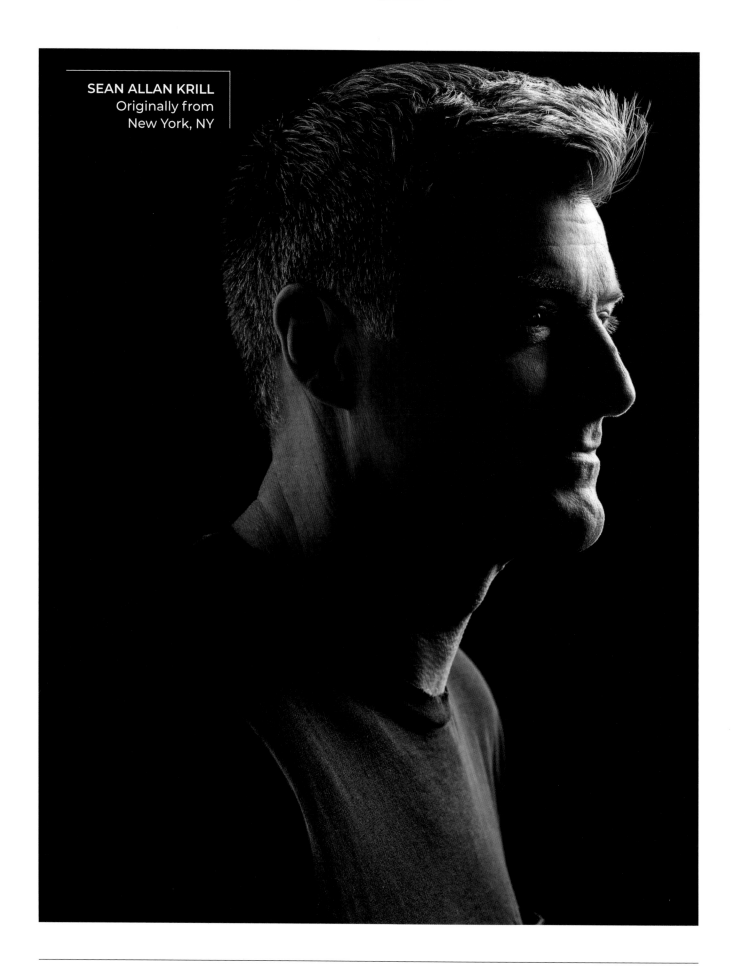

SEAN ALLAN KRILL
Originally from
New York, NY

Dear Sean,

When the lights are bright again, remember. Try to remember it all.

Remember the hundreds of thousands of lives lost; lights that can no longer shine. You were fortunate enough to live through a worldwide crisis. A plague. **And there you'll be, standing in the light of a new day. Remember to be grateful.** But also, don't forget the struggle; these feelings of helplessness, confusion, frustration, and anger toward a world that deems you non-essential and offers little help. Give these difficult emotions their due, and they can give you strength. Remember the loss, the sadness, and the solitude. In the light, it will remind you that you made it through the darkest days of the pandemic – not just because of luck, but because you struggled to be informed, resilient, compassionate, and enlightened. And you are. **You are brave and powerful.** Anyone fighting for the light is. And regardless of whether or not the world realizes its value, we are a part of something that is not only necessary for the enrichment of the human soul, but wholly and completely essential for its very survival. Art is a mirror for the world's ills, and for those who choose to look, and truly see, its reflection can heal. That's why you have to keep fighting now, through the darkness. And when the lights are bright again you can bask in their glow and know you helped to bring them back. In the wake of all we've been through, the world needs the light now more than ever.

Onward, Forward, Up,
Sean
@seanallankrill
Originally from New York, NY

Dear Bailey,

When the lights are bright again, this past year will fade into the background, but not be forgotten. This pandemic has taken so much from you and from everyone you know and love. This pandemic has also given you more than you could have ever imagined possible. Time to reflect, to compose, to live in a different way and love stronger than you ever thought your heart capable.

Everyone will rise stronger than before; if not for themselves, then for the ones we have lost far too soon. Let their sacrifice and the loss be a lesson to live every day to the fullest...when the lights are bright again.

Love Always,
Bailey
@markbaileycapalbo
Originally from New York, NY

> **You are brave and powerful. Anyone fighting for the light is.**

Dear Arnold,

When the lights are bright again…The Magic will begin anew.

We shall have what we've always had

…like when CYNTHIA ERIVO performed "I'm Beautiful" in *The Color Purple*, awakening us to the indomitable human spirit, bringing an audience to its feet in the middle of the show!

…like when JAN MAXWELL broke every rule in *Follies* by escalating to a dramatic apex in the scene preceding, "Could I Leave You?" and then from a place that would leave most actresses with nowhere to go, soared above the emotional stratosphere evoking new sensations in us!

…like when ANN HARADA enabled us to boisterously laugh at who we are, while subtly guiding us to take a deeper look at ourselves in *Avenue Q*;

…like when REBECCA LUKER with the voice of a siren and the heart of an angel made us fall in Love with Love in the *Hal Prince Show Boat* which, as Casting Director, I got to see over a hundred times;

…like STRITCH and AUDRA and LILLIAS and CAROLEE!

…like DONNA MURPHY and CHRIS JACKSON and LIN-MANUEL!

…like GRETHA BOSTON earning her Tony Award for redefining history

> **Rejuvenated from this profound respite, our own voyage shall begin…**

and CHITA for defining our history!

…and HEATHER HEADLEY and DANNY BURSTEIN and MANDY GONZALEZ and NICK CORDERO…

Some of whom we'll never see again and some of whom we cannot WAIT to see again!

…only Better!

It is not they, but we who shall be better because we will now take nothing for granted!

…Better able to hear and see and appreciate the unique ephemeral gift the Theater offers us to be in a room for a night with people who are, like all of us, only here for a moment,

Yet change us in that moment and forever!

And teach us to live anew! And better!

I thank God for every one of them.

And I cannot wait to see them, please God, even just one more time –

Changing the World.

In the words of Marcel Proust, "The real voyage of discovery consists not in seeking new landscapes, but in having new eyes."

Rejuvenated from this profound respite, our own voyage shall begin…

when the lights are bright again!

XXOO,
Arnold J. Mungioli, Casting Director
@GratefulReadyOpenWilling
Originally from New York, NY

Dear Alex,

When the lights are bright again you will cry tears of joy as you walk into the Sondheim Theatre to be reunited with your *Doubtfire* family. Your station will look just as you left it over a year ago, because for some reason you could never bring yourself to go collect your things. At first because you were sure it would be "just a couple months longer." Then it began to feel like a mini rebellion… "No one will force me to leave this theatre."

When the shutdown hit we were 3 previews into our new Broadway show. Along with navigating the profound loss we were going through as a nation, I found it almost unbearable to face the losses that effected our industry, and my personal losses that went along with it….so I didn't. In fact, I spent the early days of quarantine planning for a life WITHOUT theatre. I dove into my podcast - Pull It Together, backpacked the Pacific Northwest, **and tried to convince myself that I wanted something different. And maybe in some ways I did.**

But as time went on, it became clear, a huge part of me was missing. I've always identified as a performer, but not necessarily as an "artist." This year, because I couldn't create in the way I was used to, I was forced to explore more intimate practices of creativity. Dancing with my boyfriend in the living room because it made me feel loved and alive, and not because I wanted a job. Singing because it reminded me to breathe. Reading because it allowed me to escape, and dream. And a strange thing began to happen…I began to feel like this artist I never really identified with. A true co-creator with the universe. For this, I will forever be grateful.

> "...I found it almost unbearable to face the losses that effected our industry..."

Last week, I allowed myself to dream of returning to Broadway. I actually panicked for a moment and thought **"I hope I don't forget everything I learned this year. I hope I never forget how grateful I am to do what I love."** It's so easy as artist to get wrapped up in our productivity. This year reminded me that being a creative is more than what you do, its how you live. It's the lens through which we see the world.

Alex, when the lights are bright again you will feel more honored than you can possibly imagine to be doing what you love. You will feel flooded with joy (and probably some fear). And you will feel home.

Stay strong,
Alex
@alexandramatteo
Originally from Overland Park, KS

KEVIN RAPONEY
Originally from
Bristol, CT

> " ... never let your emotions get the best of you; remembering what it felt like when all of it disappeared unexpectedly. "

Dear Kevin,

When the lights are bright again, I hope you don't forget the feeling of them hitting your face that first time back on stage. I hope you never take a single performance for granted and always remain thankful for those moments. When dealt with hard times, I hope you remain kind and never let your emotions get the best of you; remembering what it felt like when all of it disappeared unexpectedly. **Keep working hard and never give up on your dreams.** Push yourself to meet the goals you set for yourself and always remember that we aren't promised anything in this life. Treat every day as your last. Be a good person. Stay humble.

Love always and forever,
Kevin
@raponey

Dear K,

when the lights are bright again, will you remember:

to wake each morning with a grateful heart?

to count your blessings, and not take this life and the gifts you've been given for granted?

to strive to live authentically?

to show up for yourself? to do the same for others?

to continue to do the work? to grow? to learn and unlearn?

to recognize and break, no shatter, the old patterns that have kept you from moving forward?

to set boundaries?

to speak up and to listen?

to continue to take space when and where you need to?

to take the time to truly tend to and care for your body, your mind, your heart?

to remember you are human and promise to be gracious and gentle with yourself when you fall short?

to have fun freely without constant fear?

to take risks freely without constant worry?

to feel freely without self-judgement?

to love freely without self-sabotage?

to keep loving yourself with every fiber of your being?

to tell yourself daily that you are beautiful, you are worthy, you are seen and you are loved?

to continue cultivating a garden of genuine and healthy relationships?

to change the soil and allow old roots a chance to heal and flourish,

and prune out the weeds to keep your garden growing?

to remember always to tell family and friends how much you love them, and hug them whenever you can?

to remind yourself that your career on stage, while a massive part of you, does not define you?

the stage was and always will be there for you to return home to, but you survived without it.

lastly, will you promise every day to:

rediscover your joy?

rediscover your passion?

rediscover your love?

rediscover your light?

rediscover YOU?

will you remember all that you have learned when the lights were down,

and share it fiercely with the world when the lights are bright again?

look up. we're here.

K
@kdschmitty
Originally from Green Bay, WI

"will you remember all that you have learned when the lights were down, and share it fiercely with the world when the lights are bright again?"

d to leave a space for you to share your story too. Share what you've missed about the
out your community, about your job, about your family, about your identity. Use these
elebrate, proclaim, rage, lament, or grieve. There is no right way to write your letter, but
will help, a little bit, I can promise you that.

ne out of this worldwide pandemic, let us continue to pause and listen.

ose grace for others.

any privileges we may have to elevate someone hurting.

nk about our words and the power they have.

e time and space to feel every edge of our pain.

d the hope and gumption to remember, and also to move forward.

e where we were, where we stand now, and where we wish to go.

light.

e so desperately need.

Now get writing!
A

Dear _____

*When the lights are bright again...*_____

_____

_____

_____

_____

_____

_____

_____

_____

_____

_____

ANDREW NORLEN

Originally from Troutdale, Oregon, Andrew Norlen is a NYC-based artist. With a BFA from The Boston Conservatory of Music, Andrew was most recently in the closing tour company of Broadway's *Kinky Boots*. His podcast, *Everyday Heroes*, is a space where he elevates female identifying voices. Also a writer–Andrew's memoir, *Defining Brave* comes out soon!

Follow his journey **@anorlen** and subscribe at **andrewnorlen.com** to be notified of his memoir's publication.

MATTHEW MURPHY

Matthew Murphy is a New York City-based photographer specializing in theater, dance, and portrait photography. His work is featured in the books *Hamilton: The Revolution, Come From Away: Welcome to the Rock, Dear Evan Hansen: Through the Window*, and *Jagged Little Pill: You Live, You Learn*. He travels worldwide photographing productions and lives in New York with his husband and their two dogs.

Follow him **@MurphyMade** and **MurphyMade.com**

whenthelightsarebrightagain.com

Learn more about The Actors Fund: **actorsfund.org**

Acknowledgments

The Actors Fund

Applause Books

Asya Blue

Neville Brainwaith

Kat Brunner

John Cerullo

Kendall Edwards

The Ensemblist

Scott Frost

Catalina Gaglioti

Tyler Gustin

Michael Jorgensen

Ilana Keller

KZ

Corinne Louie

Mitch Matyas

Cindy Norlen

Donnie Norlen

Ryan Scott Oliver

Stephanie Thornton Plymale

Blake Price

Lisa Price & The Price Group

Spencer Proffer

Douglas Ramirez

Valentina Ramirez-Cruz

Michaelah Reynolds

Benjamin Rivera

Kaela Salaz

MiMi Scardulla

SLIC

Kellen Stancil

Kelsee Sweigard

Jenny Taylor

Kenna Williams

Evan Zimmerman

Index

You are not alone.

Your voice matters.

Your feelings are valid.

Your dreams are possible.

You are enough.